ANTHONY MALCOMSON was educated at Campt
Emmanuel College, Cambridge. He was awarde
Queen's University, Belfast in 1970 and elected MRIA in 1987. Most of his
working life was spent in the Public Record Office of Northern Ireland, of
which he was director from 1988 until his retirement in 1998. Since then he
has devoted himself to full-time research and writing. He has published
numerous articles on Irish political and social history, and is the author of
John Foster: the Politics of the Anglo-Irish Ascendancy (Oxford, 1978); *The
Pursuit of the Heiress: aristocratic Marriage in Ireland, 1750–1820* (Belfast,
1982) and, most recently, *Archbishop Charles Agar, Churchmanship and
Politics in Ireland, 1760–1810* (Four Courts Press, Dublin, 2002). He is
currently completing a book, to be published in 2005, entitled 'Nathaniel
Clements: Government and the governing *Elite* in Ireland, *c.* 1725–*c.* 1775'.

Bust of Primate Robinson, 1770,
by John Bacon the elder (1740–99), which stands in
the library of Robinson's Oxford college,
Christ Church, and is reproduced by courtesy of the Dean.

Primate Robinson

1709–94

*'a very tough incumbent,
in fine preservation'*

A.P.W. MALCOMSON

ULSTER HISTORICAL
FOUNDATION

First published 2003
by the Ulster Historical Foundation
12 College Square East, Belfast BT1 6DD
www.ancestryireland.com

The Ulster Historical Foundation is pleased to acknowledge
support for this publication given by Armagh City
and District Council.

© A.P.W. Malcomson
ISBN 1-903688-33-7

Printed by ColourBooks Ltd, Dublin
Design by Dunbar Design

In memory of
Michael Goodall
1956–2002

CONTENTS

LIST OF ILLUSTRATIONS

SECTION I

Sir Thomas Robinson, 1st Bt (1700–77)
of Rokeby Park, Yorkshire, Primate Robinson's eldest brother.

Mrs Elizabeth Montagu (*née* Robinson)
Primate Robinson's favourite cousin.

George Stone, archbishop of Armagh, 1747–63,
Robinson's patron and predecessor.

Hugh Smithson Percy, 2nd Earl and 1st Duke of Northumberland,
the lord lieutenant under whose auspices Robinson became primate.

John Russell, 4th Duke of Bedford,
the lord lieutenant who thought Robinson was a 'rascal'.

George Nugent Grenville, 3rd Earl Temple
and 1st Marquess of Buckingham, lord lieutenant,
1782–3 and 1787–9.

Charles Agar, Archbishop of Cashel.

General Henry Robinson, 6th and last Lord Rokeby.

SECTION II

Primate Robinson, 1763.

Part of Canterbury quadrangle, Christ Church College, Oxford.

Side-elevation of the Robinson, or Armagh Public, Library.

Bookplate of Primate Robinson, 1769.

John Hotham, bishop of Clogher, 1782–95.

John Rocque's *Plan of the City of Armagh*, 1760.

Garden front of The Palace, Armagh.

The chapel built by Robinson near the west end
of The Palace, 1781–6.

Primate Robinson, 1775.

FOREWORD

ARCHBISHOP ROBIN EAMES

AMONG HISTORIANS Primate Robinson has provoked varied estimates as to his importance as an ecclesiastical leader, parliamentarian, social reformer and benefactor. In the Armagh of today tourists are reminded of his many building exploits including the Palace, the Royal School and the Observatory. Reference is frequently made to his contribution to social advancement at a formative period of the ecclesiastical capital of Ireland. In most instances such references speak in terms of affirmation, even in responses of historical achievement approaching a sense of awe.

Anthony Malcomson presents a different picture of this complex character. In this monograph we read of Robinson's 'feebleness and evasiveness as a political leader', his 'aloofness from the turbulent and increasingly sectarian politics of Co. Armagh' and his 'abandonment' of leadership in the Church of Ireland during his later years.

But it is in relationship to his dealings with that other cult figure of ecclesiastical Irish history, Archbishop Agar, that Malcomson portrays much of the vicissitudes of Robinson's character. The advancement of Agar presented Robinson with a dilemma which he never resolved – and finally despite his strenuous efforts to prevent – eclipsed Robinson as a Church and community leader.

These pages present a closely argued case for a reassessment of Primate Robinson's significance in Irish history which is in contrast to the oft-quoted credit attributed to 'the builder of Armagh'.

† Robert Armagh
DECEMBER 2003

ACKNOWLEDGEMENTS
AND
INTRODUCTION

RICHARD ROBINSON, the sixth son of William Robinson of Rokeby Park, Greta Bridge, Yorkshire, was archbishop of Armagh 1765–94, and for his political services was created Baron Rokeby in the peerage of Ireland in 1777. While scholars and specialists will, as always, have different ideas, to most people of moderate historical awareness 'Primate Robinson' is the only archbishop of Armagh who is anything like a household name. This has much to do with Arthur Young's celebrated account of his visit to Robinson's Armagh in 1776, and with the number of still functioning buildings and institutions which bear Robinson's name or mark. Whether it also rests on achievements of a less vicarious kind is a question worth asking and perhaps overdue an answer. There is no surviving Robinson archive. But there is sufficient new or untapped evidence about him, some of it in print but most in manuscript, to make possible the reassessment of Robinson which this monograph attempts.

My interest in Robinson was aroused in the course of my recent research for the book which emerged as *Archbishop Charles Agar: Churchmanship and Politics in Ireland, 1760–1810* (Dublin, 2002). Over and over again, I found that these two pre-eminent ecclesiatics were *doppelgänger*; more surprisingly, I found that the career of Robinson, who was much the senior of the two and the older by a generation, was overshadowed by that of Agar, to the point of eventual eclipse. Meanwhile, because more people, especially in the north of Ireland, had heard of Robinson than had heard of Agar, and were interested in learning more about him, I found myself 'mugging up' on Robinson as a separate study in his own right, so that I could respond to invitations to talk about him to a variety of organisations and groups. In particular, the present monograph is a derivative from papers on Robinson which I read to the Markethill and District Historical Society in September 2000 and to the Armagh Diocesan Historical Society in March 2001. Basically, it is a reworking and/or expansion of sections of *Archbishop Charles Agar*. But, although there is considerable overlap between the two, the focus is quite different. In the book, Agar is the central figure and Robinson only an important also-ran; in the present monograph I have brought together all the material relating to Robinson, have gone into greater detail when necessary and have rewritten the resulting text as a biographical essay on Robinson.

My first acknowledgement is to the various friends and colleagues who invited me to speak and/or encouraged me to put my thoughts into publishable form, particularly to Sir Peter Froggatt, Dr Eoin Magennis, Mr Neil McGleenon, Monsignor Raymond Murray, Dr R.W. Strong and Mr Roger Weatherup. The Rev. Dr W.G. Neely kindly read the text in draft and made helpful comments, though I do not mean by this to inculpate him in some of my more severe strictures on his bygone diocesan. (Canon Neely's own rectory in Keady, Co. Armagh, is incidentally a good surviving example of a building mainly sponsored by Robinson.) I am grateful to Four Courts Press, Dublin, the publishers of *Archbishop Charles Agar*, for allowing me to publish this monograph while *Archbishop Charles Agar* is still in print. I wish also to thank the Most Rev. The Lord Eames, Archbishop of Armagh, for providing a pithy preface.

My next acknowledgement is to the owners and/or depositors of manuscript material drawn upon in the present study. The biggest single source is the Normanton (i.e. Agar) papers, Hampshire Record Office, 21 M 57, which have been selectively photocopied by the Public Record Office of Northern Ireland, T/3719. In all cases where there is a PRONI photocopy, I have cited it in preference to the Hampshire RO original. I am grateful to the present Earl of Normanton and the County Archivist of Hampshire for permission to draw on the Normanton papers, and to the Deputy Keeper of the Records, PRONI, for permission to draw on these and other manuscript sources cited hereafter.

I would also like to record my gratitude to the following individuals and institutions, whose respective contributions are explained in the endnotes: Mr Sean Bardon of the Armagh County Museum; Dr T.C. Barnard; Mr Isaac Beattie of the Palace Stables Heritage Centre, Armagh; the Bedfordshire and Luton Record Office and Mr O.C.R. Wynne (in respect of the Primate Stuart papers); the British Library Board; Professor B.M.S. Campbell; Ms Nova Carlson of the General Reference Section, Belfast Public Library; the Very Rev. Herbert Cassidy, Dean of Armagh and Librarian of (Robinson's foundation) the Armagh Public Library; Miss Pamela Clark, Registrar, the Royal Archives, Windsor; Mrs Judith Curthoys, Archivist, Christ Church College, Oxford, and the Dean of Christ Church; the Derbyshire Record Office (in respect of the Sir Robert Wilmot papers); the Most Rev. The Lord Eames, Archbishop of Armagh, and the Diocesan Registrar of Armagh; Sir Peter Froggatt; Mr J.A. Gamble; the Viscount Harberton; the Linen Hall Library, Belfast (particularly Mr Gerry Healey and the staff of the Irish section); the Henry E. Huntington Library, San Marino, California; Dr James Kelly, Head of History, St Patrick's College, Drumcondra; Ms Catherine McCullough, Curator, the Armagh County Museum; Mr Peter MacDonagh; the Viscount Massereene and Ferrard; the Trustees of the National Library of Ireland; the Rev. Dr W.G. Neely; the Public Record Office, Kew; the Representative Church Body Library, Dublin; and the Earl of Shannon.

Finally, I should like to thank all those concerned with the actual production of this monograph: Mr T.D. Scott of W/P Plus, who intuitively word-processed the final draft from a succession of messy predecessors; Mr Brendan O'Brien, who made significant improvements to my text at copy-editing stage; Wendy Dunbar of Dunbar Design; Fintan Mullan and all the staff of the Ulster Historical Foundation, who were a pleasure to deal with; and the Trustees of the UHF, who were good enough to publish *Primate Robinson*.

I have dedicated it to the memory of Michael Goodall, whose death in December 2002 was a great loss to PRONI and a great sadness to everyone who knew him, through PRONI or in other connections. He had an irrepressible enthusiasm for historical research, and liked nothing better than to bring new evidence to bear on familiar themes. He also had a wicked sense of humour, and although he was a twentieth-century specialist, he enjoyed the eighteenth-century turn of phrase (for example, 'a very tough incumbent, in fine preservation'). On both counts, I hope that this is his kind of book.

A.P.W. MALCOMSON
DECEMBER 2003

ROBINSON'S PROGRESSION
TO THE PRIMACY
1751–65

———◆———

WHATEVER CLAIMS ROBINSON has to have been an extraordinary primate, he was appointed in what by 1765 had become the ordinary way. Between 1702 and 1822, the archbishopric of Armagh and Primacy of All Ireland was held by an unbroken succession of Englishmen whose remit, in addition to their ecclesiastical responsibilities, was to assist in running Ireland along lines conducive to British interests.[1] In the period 1702–65, in particular, 'ecclesiastical statesmen were almost as prominent in the government of Ireland as they had been in that of France during the seventeenth century. The lords lieutenant were largely non-resident, and during their absence the country was governed by two or three lords justices, one of whom was almost invariably the primate or an archbishop.' Following the Hanoverian Succession and the triumph of Whiggery in 1714, a bitter rivalry developed between the 'English' and the 'Irish' interests on the Irish episcopal bench. 'By 1760, the 22 bishops were divided equally between those born in Ireland and those introduced from England, with three of the four archbishops in the latter category.' When it was wittily remarked that Hugh Boulter (archbishop of Armagh, 1724–42) and Theophilus Bolton (archbishop of Cashel, 1730–44) were 'as great enemies as Christianity will permit', this was not an allusion to theological disagreement. The English-born Primate Boulter saw himself, and was seen, as the watchdog of the 'English interest' in Ireland, and he carefully stocked the Irish episcopal bench with Englishmen and kept open a hotline to the

1

British Prime Minister, Sir Robert Walpole. The Irish-born Bolton was the head of the 'Irish interest', in succession to his late patron, William King (archbishop of Dublin, 1703–29).

Boulter's not-quite-immediate successor, George Stone (archbishop of Armagh, 1747–64), was even more of a political primate. But Stone – 'that man of bustle and noisy name'[2] – was a political primate of a more controversial and objectionable kind. He descended from Boulter's Olympian heights into the arena of Irish politics and brought the primacy into more than passing disrepute. His hatreds were focused not on rival churchmen, but on his fellow party leaders in the Irish parliament, notably Henry Boyle, 1st Earl of Shannon (1682–1764), speaker of the House of Commons, 1733–56. Towards the end of Stone's life, the Co. Down magnate and British politician, the 1st Earl of Hillsborough (who will be cited in due course as an admirer of Robinson), inveighed against what he called 'the deceit and treachery and ingratitude and silly ambition of … the odious Primate'.[3] Robinson was Stone's almost exact contemporary, and they had been friends in their youth at Christ Church College, Oxford.[4]

Robinson came to Ireland in 1751 as one of the chaplains to the 1st Duke of Dorset, lord lieutenant, 1750–55. During these years, Dorset and his second son and chief secretary, Lord George Sackville, both fell under the baneful influence of Stone, who led them to defeat and discredit in a quite unnecessary power struggle with 'the Irish interest', then represented by Henry Boyle. Under Sackville/Stone patronage, Robinson's rise in the Church of Ireland was rapid – more rapid than any eighteenth-century bishop except Stone himself. Stone had been 'consecrated bishop of Ferns in 1740, translated to Kildare in 1743, to Derry in 1745, and became primate in 1747 at the exceptionally early age of thirty-nine. He owed everything to the patronage of his brother, Andrew, who as well as being the under-secretary to the English ecclesiastical Minister, the Duke of Newcastle, was also the governor of the future King George III.' The rise of Robinson was spectacular by any other standards: bishop of Killala, 1751 (the year of his arrival); bishop of Ferns, 1759; bishop of Kildare, 1761; and primate, 1765. And it, too (as will be seen), was accelerated by connections at Court. Stone had not actually started his career as a viceregal chaplain (of the eighteenth-century primates, Lindsay,

Robinson and Newcome did so, and Marsh, Boulter, Hoadly and Stone did not). But in general terms that was the single most common route of advancement. All told, forty eighteenth-century bishops – nearly all of them Englishmen – started off as 'chaplain to the lord lieutenant or some other powerful lay lord'. In 1751, when approving the elevation of Robinson to his first bishopric, George II commented sensibly: 'all the bishoprics must not be given to chaplains'.[5] But nothing was done to curtail the practice. Viceregal chaplains inhaled the political atmosphere of Dublin Castle, and usually were employed there as viceregal private secretaries. Robinson was promoted too soon to a bishopric to be used in the latter capacity. But, as late as 1778, when he had been primate for over thirteen years, he was still being categorised as 'of the Dorset House'.[6]

Dorset was recalled in 1755. In 1759, Stone successfully recommended Robinson to the then lord lieutenant, the 4th Duke of Bedford, for Robinson's next bishopric, that of Ferns.[7] As bishop of Ferns, 1759–61, Robinson endeavoured to testify to his continuing political allegiance to 'the Dorset House'. One of the cares of that bishopric was the borough of Old Leighlin, Co. Carlow, for which the bishop returned two members to the House of Commons; and Robinson claimed that he had made arrangements to fill the seats with two Sackville nominees at the forthcoming general election *before* he learned early in 1761 of his promotion, at Bedford's recommendation, to the bishopric of Kildare. It was, however, a suspicious circumstance that Bedford had just resigned the lord lieutenancy, and so could be of no further use to Robinson. With considerable effrontery, Robinson wrote to him in late March 1761 expressing the hope

> that my engagements ... for filling the borough of Leighlin ... will appear to your Grace to be agreeable to the strictest principles of probity and equity. Accounts have been received in Ireland, perhaps destitute of all foundation, that two gentlemen different from those to whom I stand engaged, will be recommended by Dr Jackson [his successor at Ferns] as candidates for Leighlin ... If it is ... expected that my engagements with persons of the first rank, honour and influence in this kingdom should be annihilated by the acceptance of the bishopric of Kildare, I do not see that I can at this time accept that bishopric thus conditioned, unless I would relinquish the comfort and credit of being esteemed an honest man the remainder of my life.[8]

Bedford was so far from esteeming Robinson an honest man in this transaction that he replied tartly: 'it did not become your Lordship to accept the recommendation to Old Leighlin from any other person whatsoever than from him who had obtained from the Crown your two last promotions, especially as at that time he was honoured with His Majesty's Commission of Chief Governor of Ireland'.[9] Robinson, by contrast, had regarded himself as being at liberty to oblige his original patron, the Duke of Dorset, and through him Primate Stone, and Stone's and Dorset's ally, John Ponsonby, speaker of the House of Commons (in succession to Henry Boyle), 1756–71. Stone and Ponsonby were the 'persons of the first rank, honour and influence in this kingdom' referred to in Robinson's letter, and were at this time using their position as lords justices in Bedford's absence to thwart his wishes and curry popularity in Ireland.[10]

The dispute soon became a *cause célèbre* not only in Dublin, but in Whitehall and St James's. Bedford's chief secretary, Richard Rigby, who currently sat for Old Leighlin, also inveighed against Robinson and called what he had written to Bedford 'the most Jesuitical, shuffling letter I ever read in my life. Was there ever a greater rascal than this Bishop! I hope your Grace [Bedford] will be of opinion with me that the sooner Jackson goes to Ireland, the better, for it will be horrid provoking to have this villain get this additional preferment from you, at the very instant when he is flying in your face in the last see to which you promoted him.'[11] The new bishop, Jackson, who was a Bedfordshire protégé of the Duke and one of his viceregal chaplains, naturally endorsed the ducal sentiments, and called Robinson's letter 'such an ungrateful one … as I could not have expected to have come from any man, much less one of his rank and order'.[12] Robinson now realised that he had over-stepped the mark, and was fearful of incurring the displeasure of the King. He therefore wrote to his younger brother, General Sir Septimus Robinson, who had been governor of two of George III's younger brothers, the Dukes of Gloucester and Cumberland, 1751–60, and was now gentleman usher of the Black Rod[13] (circumstances of considerable importance for the future), in an effort to rehabilitate himself. 'The letter from Bishop Robinson to his brother, Sep.,' wrote Rigby, 'was no other than a copy of his elaborate epistle to the Duke of Bedford. Sep. showed it to Lord

Waldegrave [governor of George III, as prince of Wales, 1752–6] and others, who all abused the performance and its author as much as I have done, but not so much as I will do when the election at Leighlin is over.' Finally, Robinson read his 'recantation'[14] and Bedford's two nominees were returned for Old Leighlin.

Between 1761 and Stone's death in December 1764, Robinson continued to court and follow him, turning a blind eye to Stone's enormities, of which addiction to political intrigue was not the greatest.

> The Primate of Ireland ... had every vice but hypocrisy, [and] took every shape but that of a man of virtue and religion: polite, insinuating, generous, the pimp of pleasure and the spy of state, a slave to one vice, but the other vices, especially the most natural one, he made to serve his purposes. Had he been galant [sic], he could have obliged but one lady at a time, but from his own seraglio he obtained many. He governed private families by providing the ladies with lovers of his own educating. They were taught by his Lordship to spell the love letters they wrote. This prelate was much such a successor to St Patrick as Pope Sixtus to St Peter.[15]

The writer of these withering words, the famous bluestocking, Mrs Elizabeth Montagu (née Robinson), was Robinson's favourite cousin, who went to see him every year at Bath or Bristol, where he spent much of the long Irish parliamentary recess.[16] So there can be no doubt about the source of her information. According to Horace Walpole, Stone's constant political entertaining had made him 'a sacrifice to drunkenness, which, however, was but a libation to ambition'. Walpole was prone to sensationalisation. But in this instance he was drawing on an eyewitness account of Stone's dinner-parties in his palatial house in Henrietta Street, Dublin, where 'the rake took the place of the archbishop'.[17] In spite of all this, Robinson stuck to Stone (and, in 1765, perpetuated the association by taking on the lease of the Henrietta Street house, scene and symbol of the latter's Dublin debaucheries). It was through Stone's – and other political – influence that he rose in the Church and eventually was made primate. As has been drily observed: 'Robinson, it would seem, achieved little of any real importance in the three bishoprics which he held before the Primacy'.[18] Something similar was said, in a more convoluted way, at the time of his promotion to Armagh. His appointment 'was not owing to any interest that ought to have contributed to it. The qualities of the successor [to Stone] are ... in all points (except ability) the same as those of his predecessor, who is suggested to have established this extraordinary succession before he departed.'[19]

Since Robinson was Stone's protégé and candidate for the primacy, it might be thought that the widespread revulsion at Stone in December 1764 would have operated against Robinson's pretensions to succeed him. The lord lieutenant of the day, the 1st Earl, later 1st Duke, of Northumberland, who was to contribute materially to the appointment of Robinson, spoke 'of the Primate's death rather with pleasure than regret, and ... [has] found him out in a thousand tricks ... The conversation of my Lord Lieutenant's family is ... that business will go on much better when the Primate is dead and when my Lord Lieutenant takes everything under his own management.'[20] So Northumberland, for one, would never have acted on Stone's advice unless there were other circumstances favouring Robinson. The most important of these was Sir Septimus Robinson's position in the royal household, the princess dowager's attachment to him, Lord Bute's attachment to the princess dowager, and Northumberland's attachment to Lord Bute. Another important circumstance was George III's bad relations with the ministry of the day, headed by George Grenville,[21] who favoured candidates other than Robinson. Horace Walpole commented: 'I do not think the Administration will be disposed to place the Metropolitan mitre on an able head again in haste; and I am sure, in that case, they will have little difficulty to furnish themselves to their minds from the English Bench, whence I hear the choice is to be made.'[22] In fact, Grenville *did* want an able man, but someone who would act as a representative of the British government, not an Irish politician, a dignified and detached Boulter-figure, not a 'noxious and troublesome' party-man.[23] To Thomas Newton, bishop of Bristol, he wrote asking him to accept the primacy, 'always to be one of the Lords Justices, constantly to correspond with him [Grenville, and] to give him certain intelligence of everything material'.[24]

Newton was actually his second choice, his first having been Edmund Keene, bishop of Chester; but both declined. This, too, came to the ears of Walpole, who hated Grenville and commented gleefully:

> Mr Grenville, believing himself possessed of power because he runs all the risk of it, offered the Archiepiscopal mitre about the town, without remembering to ask if it was in his disposal. Two English Bishops declined it. Lord Granby then solicited for his tutor, Ewer of Llandaff, and was supported by the imaginary Minister. But the *Lord Lieutenant* (the most acute commentators read *Lord Bute*) carried off the Primacy for Robinson, Bishop of Kildare. The Duke of Bedford, still more a phantom than Grenville, imagined he could obtain the nomination, and demanded it for a Scoto-Hibernian, Bishop Carmichael.[25]

Bedford, the lord president of the council in the Grenville administration, and on close terms with the Prime Minister, was understandably anxious to keep out Robinson. However, the Hon. William Carmichael, a Scotsman on the Irish bench, was a perfectly creditable candidate, and as bishop of Meath since 1758, was much senior to Robinson. Walpole's letter is presumably the authority for the *DNB*'s statement that Robinson was appointed 'contrary to the wishes of … Grenville, who brought forward three nominees of his own'. This is somewhat misleading. Grenville, in his diary, recorded that the King 'seemed to approve' of Keene of Chester. When Newton of Bristol was mentioned to him, the King 'did not disapprove it, but seemed more inclined to Dr Robinson'. When both Keene and Newton declined, Grenville does not record that he proposed Bishop Ewer, in spite of Lord Granby's earnestness on Ewer's behalf. Nor does he mention his response to Bedford's recommendation of Carmichael. From this it would seem that Grenville actually named only two people to the King, Keene and Newton, and that the first, probably, and the second, possibly, would have become primate if both had not declined. Grenville's diary entry concludes: 'The King pauses upon appointing anyone to it as yet, and in that and some other instances of delays … and averseness to what Mr Grenville proposes … he [Grenville] feels the effects of some inferior persons who get about His Majesty, and seemingly indispose him to his Principal Servants'.[26]

This was of course what happened. Robinson's 'extraordinary succession' to the archbishopric of Armagh, 'the first and richest in

Ireland, and perhaps richer than any in England',[27] was as much a 'Bedchamber Plot' as his patron, Stone's, had been in 1747, with the aggravation in Robinson's case that it also owed something to his condoning of Stone's vices. Northumberland's support (which Robinson acknowledged years later, in 1782, by erecting an obelisk to him in the park of the recently completed Armagh Palace) was also no credit to Robinson; it had earlier been remarked that Northumberland's episcopal appointments proved that he was not 'a connoisseur in bishops'.[28] One Irish MP who had belonged to Stone's political following quipped in January 1765 that 'part of the Ministry were for having a good politician, part for a good churchman, and in the end they have chosen neither'.[29] This was a harsh verdict, particularly in relation to the good things which Robinson was to do for the Church in the early years of his primacy. But, in relation to Robinson's previous record and to the events of December 1764–January 1765, it is hard to accept the view 'that his appointment marked a deliberate move to have a primate who would concentrate on Church rather than political affairs'.[30] Ten years earlier, when asked to advise on the filling of the vacant governorship of Virginia, the Lord Chancellor of England, Lord Hardwicke, had observed that the office could either be given to an efficient public servant who would reside in the colony or be 'disposed of in a Court way'. In 1765, the archbishopric of Armagh was 'disposed of in a Court way'.[31]

THE PRIMATE IN HIS PRIME
1765–78

———————————◆———————————

WHAT HAS BEEN CALLED 'The Era of graceful Reform, 1800–1830'[32] in the Church of Ireland had uneven and almost imperceptible (except that they came much earlier than 1800) beginnings; and it was in the nature of things, since the reformers came from within, that they should be products of a system of promotion which was itself in need of reformation. Robinson was a case in point. From inauspicious, even suspicious, beginnings, he made a considerable mark in his first twelve or so years in the primacy. In spite of his 'Jesuitical' past, he proved to be the antithesis of his patron, Stone – a contrast which greatly enhanced his standing. The chief symptom of a recrudescence of the old party-political Robinson came in 1768, when he returned Sir George Macartney for the borough of Armagh, which was 'annexed to the Primacy',[33] just as Old Leighlin was annexed to Ferns. By a happy coincidence, Macartney was by then chief secretary to the lord lieutenant and therefore a choice of member which was welcome to Dublin Castle. But Robinson had originally promised to return Macartney at the request of Northumberland,[34] long before Macartney was even under consideration for the post of chief secretary. In other words, Robinson still stuck to his partisan interpretation of the obligations which bound a bishop who had *ex officio* responsibility for a borough.

It could be argued that, in other respects also, Robinson was not a changed man, and that he had little choice but to abjure politics and concentrate on his ecclesiastical concerns. His influence at Court declined rapidly, with the death of his brother, Sir Septimus, later in

1765, the waning of the influence of Lord Bute, and the death of the princess dowager in 1772.[35] The only welcome development, from Robinson's point of view, was the appointment in 1771 of 'Sep.'s' former charge, the Duke of Gloucester, as chancellor of Dublin University, following the death of Robinson's old enemy, Bedford; this was potentially important to Robinson, who was heavily involved with the affairs of the university as its vice-chancellor (since 1765) and as one of the College Visitors.[36] Another development in Court and Cabinet which was of definite advantage to him was the appointment of Stone's and his old patron, Lord George Sackville (who had by now changed his name to Germain), as secretary of state for the colonies in 1775. In more general terms, however, Robinson's first decade in the primacy coincided with a conscious change of government policy, whereby authority was 'brought back to the Castle' (as the contemporary phrase ran), the lord lieutenant became full-time resident from 1767 onwards, and the need to appoint the primate or any other prominent figure as a lord justice ceased to exist unless under exceptional circumstances. These, in fact, arose only twice between Robinson's enthronement as primate and his death.[37] The first occasion was between 27 October and 16 December 1787, following the sudden death in office of the 4th Duke of Rutland, and the second – and much more important, because it lasted longer and involved some important decisions – was between 25 June 1789 and 5 January 1790, following the 1st Marquess of Buckingham's nervous collapse as a result of the Regency Crisis. On both occasions, Robinson was one of three *ex officio* lords justices appointed (the others being the lord chancellor and the speaker of the House of Commons); on both, he was – and remained – in England. This was a striking contrast to the behaviour of Stone, who would have embraced Islam sooner than forgo service on the commission of lords justices. Otherwise, Robinson was a stranger to even quasi-political office – so much so that, when appointed a trustee of the linen manufacture (a numerous body and by no means a rare distinction) in 1777, he could state without conscious irony that membership of that board was 'out of the line of my profession'.[38]

Because he toed such a line (at least ostensibly), his 'political conduct' deserved, in the tribute paid him by the outgoing lord lieutenant, the 1st Earl Harcourt, in 1776, 'the highest encomium that can be given to it. He is an enemy to all intrigue and faction. His only object is the King's service and the honourable support of his government.'[39] In a well-known letter of January 1777, the already-mentioned Lord Hillsborough (who, incidentally, held in common with Robinson a strong admiration of the church organs built by John Snetzler) described Robinson to the new lord lieutenant, the 2nd Earl of Buckinghamshire, 'as one of the best men living. He is a man of very sound judgement and what is better of a very sound heart, a true friend to the dignity and interest of Government, and has effected more for the civilisation and improvement of Ireland than any ten men for these hundred years. He hates and despises a job, and whatever information he gives you I will venture to say you may depend upon.'[40] Buckinghamshire soon came to a similar conclusion:

> The Primate of Ireland, of all the churchman I ever knew in any country, does the most honour to his profession, happy in the talents of reconciling ease with dignity, and of blending the strictest attention to the respectable duties of the situation with the amiable qualities of society, and no otherwise interfering in the tumultuous politics of this country than to give a decent support to the interests of England, and to testify a becoming gratitude to that government from whence he derived the consequence of those emoluments which he so respectably enjoys.[41]

Unquestionably, Robinson in his first dozen years as primate and as *ex officio* treasurer to the board of first fruits had many positive achievements to his credit as a builder and improver, an administrator at diocesan, metropolitan and primatial level, a legislator, and an enforcer of lapsed ecclesiastical standards. Examples of this last are his refusal to consecrate men as bishops who were below the episcopal age of thirty, or the rule he 'laudably laid down for himself' never to grant any clergyman a faculty to hold more than two pieces of preferment at the one time.[42] Sometimes the two pieces of preferment were impossibly far apart,[43] but this was a reflection of the then low value of many livings and the need to combine them in order to provide adequate remuneration for clergymen, rather than of laxity on the part of Robinson. The discretion to authorise or forbid pluralities lay exclusively with the primate – the other three archbishops did not exercise it within their respective provinces, nor did the bishops exercise it within their respective dioceses[44] – so it gave Robinson the means of effecting a country-wide improvement. In his day, he was credited with the maxim 'that the first step towards civilisation is a resident clergy'[45] (although one resident clergyman of Robinson's province, Philip Skelton, quipped that Robinson 'was very careful to build churches, but did not care what sort of clergymen he put in them').[46] '[Bishop Richard] Mant in his *History of the Church of Ireland* quotes from an edition of *Anthologia Hibernica* which reads: "No Primate ever sat in the See of Armagh, who watched more carefully over the interests of the Church of Ireland, as the statute book evinces"'; and D.A. Chart, taking up this theme, writes: 'to his general church administration the statute book of the Irish Parliament during his twenty-nine years of office (1765–94) bears witness'.[47]

Some of these assertions require modification. Three-quarters of the sixteen acts of parliament which Robinson sponsored over the period 1758–84 were concentrated on the period 1768–76, during those fruitful first twelve years of his primacy. Although he later claimed that he had been present at the start of every session of parliament between 1751 and 1785,[48] he did not set foot in the House of Lords after September 1785 and left Ireland, never to return, in October 1786; so the last nine years of his primacy may be deducted from the twenty-nine mentioned by Chart. During his first twenty years he 'attended very regularly', being present for 'approximately 545' meetings of the House.[49] But attendance was measured on the basis of who was present for prayers (a very episcopal avocation) at the beginning of each day's sitting, not on the basis of who was there for all or most of the day. Moreover, attendance in this period was not unduly onerous, since parliament met, generally speaking, for only six months in every two years until 1784. In the intervening periods of a year and a half, Robinson was free to attend to his diocese and metropolitan province and, more to the point, go to London, Bath or 'some other English pool of Bethesda'.[50] These prolonged absences in England should not be regarded as a matter of course: in 1765, Thomas Newton, one of the two English bishops who had been offered the primacy ahead of Robinson and had declined it, stated that, 'if he had accepted … it was his firm resolution to become a perfect

Irishman … never to entertain a thought of returning even upon a visit to England, but … there [Ireland] to have passed and ended his days'.[51] Two years later, the anonymous author of an update of Thomas Prior's famous *List of the Absentees of Ireland* endorsed Newton's view by placing Robinson 'in the shameful catalogue of absentees'.[52]

The question now arises: who, if not Robinson, was responsible for much of the ecclesiastical legislation of the period *c*.1780 onwards which 'the statute book evinces'? The answer, in the main, is Charles Agar, bishop of Cloyne, 1768–79; archbishop of Cashel, 1779–1801; and archbishop of Dublin, 1801–9. Very conveniently, both Robinson and Agar have left lists of the legislative enactments for which they were respectively responsible.[53] Of the sixteen acts which Robinson sponsored, one made its predecessor perpetual and one amended another. In addition, one of Robinson's acts (7 Geo. III, c. 21) had to be amended by Agar's 35 Geo. III, c. 32, which was an Act 'To explain 3 Geo. III, c. 25, and 7 Geo. III, c. 21, viz. the summary Tithe Law'. Up to the Union, Agar credited himself with fourteen acts and two clauses, the earlier of the two clauses being sec. 17 of Robinson's Act of 1772 for the 'erecting of new Chapels of Ease in Parishes of large Extent' in the diocese of Armagh and elsewhere (11 & 12 Geo. III, c. 16). The slight overlap between Robinson's and Agar's legislation may have caused Mant and Chart to attribute a number of pre-1794 measures to Robinson when in fact they were the handiwork of Agar. The list of Robinson's acts is almost certainly exhaustive: the list of Agar's is not, because Agar erred on the side of understatement. He seems to have *excluded* some ten acts to which he was a major contributor, but of which he was not the sole author – for example, two of the anti-Rightboy measures of 1787 in favour of the clergy (27 Geo. III, c. 36 and 40).[54] Robinson may not have been the sole author of any of the acts listed as his, for the good reason that he enjoyed, for almost the whole of his primacy, the expert assistance of two veteran ecclesiastical administrators and diocesan officials, Henry Upton, the diocesan and provincial registrar of Armagh, and Henry Meredyth, the agent for the archiepiscopal estate, a former Dublin Castle official and an MP for Armagh borough, 1776–89.[55] Agar enjoyed no such back-up. Significantly, the list of Robinson's acts is in Upton's handwriting, while the list of Agar's is in Agar's own.

However, the most important difference between Robinson's and Agar's acts is that the former were almost all local to the diocese of Armagh and/or uncontroversial, while the latter were general and almost always involved a high level of political difficulty, particularly when it came to getting them through the House of Commons. Even Robinson's ostensibly general acts had a strong local imperative. His last measure, passed in 1784 (23 & 24 Geo. III, c. 49), 'An Act for making appropriate Parishes belonging to Archbishops and Bishops perpetual Cures, and the better to enable such Archbishops and Bishops to endow and augment the Endowments of Vicarages and Curacies [therein]', was partly inspired by his generous intentions in regard to the Co. Louth part of his diocese (see below). Likewise, his Act of 1772 'for rendering more effectual the several Laws for the better enabling of the Clergy, having Cure of Souls, to reside upon their Benefices, and to build upon their respective Glebes, and to prevent Dilapidations' (11 & 12 Geo. III, c. 17) had the perhaps not wholly unintentional effect of throwing the full cost of his new palace upon his unfortunate successor (see below). Typical of Robinson's legislative programme was his Act of 1772 'to prevent burying dead Bodies in Churches' (11 & 12 Geo. III, c. 22) – a useful, uncontroversial, health-and-safety measure founded on early eighteenth-century English precedent.[56]

Although only one of Agar's measures, the clause which he contributed to one of Robinson Acts of 1772, fell within the twelve-year period which has been characterised as Robinson's prime, for part of that period Agar was in other respects establishing his pretensions to the first vacant archbishopric, and his credentials as 'infinitely the first ecclesiastic, if not the first man of business, in the House of Lords'. This was the assessment of Agar which his friend and political ally, the Irish attorney-general, John Scott, wrote for the benefit of the British Prime Minister, Lord North, in December 1778.[57] No one in Robinson's position could fail to resent the pre-eminence thus attributed to a much younger subordinate. Born in 1735, Agar was Robinson's junior by a generation. He was a man of great ability, ambition and zeal for 'graceful reform'. Most important of all, he was Irish (though with unusually good English connections through his

Sir Thomas Robinson, 1st Bt (1700–77)
of Rokeby Park, Yorkshire, Primate Robinson's eldest brother.

Reproduced from a photogravure of an original portrait of *c.*1730,
by an unknown artist.

Mrs Elizabeth Montagu (*née* Robinson)
Primate Robinson's favourite cousin.

Reproduced from an engraving of Sir Joshua Reynolds' portrait of *c.*1765,
commissioned by Primate Robinson and bequeathed by him
to the 2nd Lord Rokeby.

George Stone, archbishop of Armagh, 1747–63,
Robinson's patron and predecessor.

Reproduced from an original portrait of *c.*1750 in Christ Church College, Oxford,
by kind permission of the Dean of Christ Church.

Hugh Smithson Percy, 2nd Earl and 1st Duke of Northumberland,
the lord lieutenant under whose auspices Robinson became primate.

Reproduced from an engraving by Aliament
after a portrait of *c*.1760.

John Russell, 4th Duke of Bedford,
the lord lieutenant who thought Robinson was a 'rascal'.

Reproduced from an engraving by H. Robinson
after a portrait of *c*.1750 by Sir Joshua Reynolds.

EARL TEMPLE.

Publish'd Sept.ʳ 30, 1782 by J. Walker N.ᵒ 44 Pater-noster Row.

George Nugent Grenville, 3rd Earl Temple
and 1st Marquess of Buckingham, lord lieutenant, 1782–3 and 1787–9.

Reproduced from an engraving of 1782
when he was lord lieutenant for the first time.

Charles Agar, archbishop of Cashel.

Reproduced from a portrait of 1782 by George Romney
in Christ Church College, Oxford,
by kind permission of the Dean of Christ Church.

General Henry Robinson, 6th and last Lord Rokeby.

Reproduced from an engraving of a portrait which must date from *c.* 1860.

uncle, Welbore Ellis, a member of Lord North's government and a toady of George III). With Robinson and Agar, a re-run of the old rivalry between the English and the Irish interests was never far below the surface.[58] The rise of Agar, and the Robinson–Agar antagonism, have not so far been mentioned in any study of Robinson. But they are crucial to what happened to Robinson at the end of his first twelve productive years as primate. Contemporaries were in no doubt about their importance. A pro-Agar under-secretary in Dublin Castle wrote privately to him in early December 1778: 'you have talents which the Pri[mate] does not possess. He hates you for it and will endeavour to prevent your standing in his way.'[59] At about the same time, John Scott argued (again for the benefit of Lord North) that, if Agar were promoted to the archbishopric of Dublin, his 'abilities will keep the Primate quiet as they have hitherto diminished his Grace's infallibility and absolute sway'.[60] Later, in February 1779, the politically astute 2nd Earl of Shannon commented: 'I am satisfied that, had my neighbour [at Cloyne] succeeded ... [to the archbishopric of] Dublin, there would have been a strong junta against the Primate, and so there will when he goes to Cashel'.[61]

Earlier in his Cloyne episcopate, Agar's relationship with Robinson had been one almost of dependence. In June 1771, writing to Robinson as treasurer to the Board of First Fruits, Agar asked if Robinson could 'give me good hopes of getting' money within the next two months for the churches he wanted to build.[62] But in the course of the 1770s Agar pulled ahead of Robinson in most respects except seniority. During one of the first attempted inroads into the Penal Laws, the bill of 1772 allowing catholics to lend money to protestants on mortgage, Agar's speech in opposition to it in the House of Lords on 22 May seems to have been decisive of its defeat by the narrow margin of two votes.[63] 'The Popish Mortgage Bill' was reintroduced in the next session and (though in the end it was lost in the House of Lords in April 1774[64]) initially scraped through that House, after a strenuous debate, on 17 December 1773. Robinson headed the list of the Lords who entered a protest against the bill in the *Journals* of their House, and expressed their fears that it was 'levelled against the whole system of Popery Laws'.[65] However, Robinson's primacy among the protestors was simply a matter of

rank: Agar's papers include an autograph draft of the protest,[66] rough-
ly but essentially corresponding to the printed version, and thus
establishing that Agar was the author of the latter. By March 1774,
Agar is to be found acting as joint manager of government business
in the Lords (his colleague being a lay peer, not Robinson).[67] In 1778,
while Robinson affected to be 'liberal and temperate'[68] on the subject
of the Catholic Relief Bill – an almost total dismemberment of the
'Popery Laws' as they affected catholic landownership – Agar was the
brains behind the unsuccessful attempt to modify it and adopt a more
gradualist approach. When a clause repealing the Sacramental Test
against protestant dissenters was tacked on to it, Agar more than any
other single individual was instrumental in getting that clause sup-
pressed in the British Privy Council.

It also must have been Agar who, probably as a *quid pro quo* for the
withdrawal of episcopal opposition in the Lords to the rest of the
Relief Bill, secured the first-ever parliamentary grant (of £6,000)
towards the church-building work of the Board of First Fruits. This
was a signal achievement. The Irish government was bankrupt at the
time and no such parliamentary grant for church-building was made
in Great Britain until 1818. From 1778 onwards, Agar pursued tena-
ciously this policy of obtaining parliamentary grants for the Board,
particularly in the years 1787–9, when he succeeded in broadening
the applicability of the grants to cover not just church-building, but
almost all aspects of the Board's activities. During 1787–9, Robinson
was permanently absent in England. But, in spite of the fact that he
personally was not in the line of fire, he consistently and unadvisedly
urged Agar not to attempt anything 'new and unprecedented …
[which] in these times will certainly be opposed'.[69]

ROBINSON'S CRISIS YEAR

1778–9 [70]

IN VIEW OF ROBINSON'S EARLIER OPPOSITION to the 'Popish Mortgage Bill', a comparative side-issue, it is remarkable that he did not oppose the Catholic Relief Act of 1778 (17 & 18 Geo. III, c. 49). The Act was not a government measure, but it was favoured by Dublin Castle with increasing overtness. Robinson had already been showing a self-abasing amenability to the wishes of Buckinghamshire and his obscure and lightweight chief secretary, Richard Heron (whom Robinson described as 'a man of so respectable a character'). Plainly, he had ulterior motives. For one thing, he wanted Buckinghamshire's backing in a power struggle in which he had been engaged since the mid-1760s over TCD and which now involved the survival or otherwise of its controversial new provost, John Hely-Hutchinson. (Robinson, it should be noted, did not openly seek Buckinghamshire's backing: he disingenuously professed to seek and advise no more than official neutrality.) However, it must be suspected that Robinson's principal motive for wanting at all costs to remain on good terms with Dublin Castle was the vacancies looming in the archbishoprics both of Dublin and Cashel, and that he was being 'liberal and temperate' about the Relief Bill with a view to dishing Agar, the strongest and, from Robinson's point of view, the most threatening candidate for either of them.

As Visitor and vice-chancellor of TCD, Robinson had been endeavouring for years to reform, or perhaps just to rule, the college. He had been at loggerheads with the previous provost, Francis Andrews, since at least 1761. Andrews was a layman and a member of parliament and politician, but at least he was a fellow of the college and academically respectable. Hely-Hutchinson, an ally of Agar, who succeeded to the provostship on Andrews's death in 1774, was not a fellow and was a flagrantly political appointee. He also set out to modernise the college and refashion it in his own image. He was soon embroiled in legal and pamphlet warfare over his changes to the curriculum, his shifting of its emphasis to a more secular form of education, his favouritism towards some fellows and persecution of others, and his efforts to turn the university constituency into a Hely-Hutchinson borough. Accordingly, Robinson in conjunction with the then attorney-general, Philip Tisdall, 'determined' Hely-Hutchinson's 'ruin'. One of Robinson's protégés in TCD, Dr Patrick Duigenan, a junior fellow who became regius professor of feudal and English law in 1776, supported Robinson and Tisdall with scurrilous anti-provost compilations. The first of these was entitled *Pranceriana* – an allusion to Hely-Hutchinson's introduction of dancing lessons into the curriculum and to his 'prancing' (i.e. displays of oratory and independence) in the House of Commons. The second was entitled *Lachrymae Academicae*. At the end of April 1777, Hely-Hutchinson and Tisdall had a set-to in the law courts, during which the former called the latter an 'old scoundrel and a rascal' – words which Tisdall interpreted as a deliberate attempt to provoke him to a duel. He responded by initiating a Crown prosecution of Hely-Hutchinson for incitement to a breach of the peace. Though Tisdall himself died in September 1777, the prosecution rumbled successfully on, and did indeed threaten Hely-Hutchinson's ruin. In other words, Robinson *was* deeply embroiled in 'the tumultuous politics' of Ireland, though one of his partisans (no doubt primed by the Primate) kept assuring Buckinghamshire of the contrary. This partisan was Richard Cumberland, the dramatist and minor diplomat (whose father had been an Irish bishop and a friend of Robinson). He assured Chief Secretary Heron in April 1777 that Robinson's 'motives are truly and uniformly public-spirited'; Robinson was concerned only for the 'interests and discipline of the University … a question of much public importance', because TCD was in need of 'a thorough reform'.

Agar's uncle, Welbore Ellis, now entered the fray on the side of

Hely-Hutchinson. By the autumn of 1778, the prosecution of the latter had reached the court of King's Bench in England, where Ellis busied himself officiously in getting it stopped. Early in November 1778, he reported to Agar that he had carried this point, 'under the condition of his [Hely-Hutchinson's] asking it as a favour of the Castle'. Hely-Hutchinson must have agreed to go through this motion. So, Robinson turned next to the chancellor of the university, the Duke of Gloucester. But the Duke, having in an unguarded moment 'very graciously received ... [Dr Duigenan] and promised him a Visitation', took avoiding action and declined to be involved.[71] This meant that, now more than ever before, the choice of the next archbishop of Dublin was crucial to the struggle over TCD. That archbishop was another of the Visitors, and the dying Archbishop Cradock had been censured by Duigenan in *Lachrymae Academicae* for allegedly favouring Hely-Hutchinson. For this reason, Hely-Hutchinson wrote to Agar in late November declaring his 'official interest in being placed under your Lordship's immediate protection'. John Scott gave dramatic expression to the consequences of appointing

> an humble slave of the Primate's [as archbishop of Dublin and] as a Visitor of our University. [It] will again throw everything there into tumult and confusion and actually rout the Provost, as well as by religious faction ruin the College to restore it to the arms of the Church ... The Provost, from the deadly hatred which subsists between the Primate and him, will do all manner of mischief ... That evil would be prevented by putting the Bishop of Cloyne to Dublin.

There was a good deal of hyperbole in this prognosis. Agar was not in the end put to Dublin, and 'the deadly hatred' between the provost and the primate subsided. As early as March 1779, Chief Secretary Heron reported to Buckinghamshire:

> The Provost is in exceeding good humour, and professes a strong desire to co-operate with the Primate, or rather to submit all regulations for the College to his Grace. He has proposed various plans which he will, if he has not already, mention to your Excellency. The Primate has reserved himself till he has the opportunity of considering the subject [i.e. discussing it with others]. The plans are

objectionable, but I assured him [Robinson?] you would be very desirous of promoting the peace of the College.[72]

The succession to Dublin in late 1778 was crucial in its own right and not just in relation to TCD; in effect, it determined whether Robinson or Agar should be the Head of the Church. Years later, in 1801, Agar was told by the able Thomas Lewis O'Beirne, Bishop of Meath:

> I have ever considered Dublin to be of more importance to morals and religion in this country than even the Primacy. The one is a place of more state and greater representation: the other, from the general influence which the manners of the capital are known to have over every other part of the kingdom, is without comparison of superior and more extensive utility, when placed in proper hands.[73]

The hands in which Robinson proposed to place it were by no means proper, and had the sole recommendation of being safely English. There was a loose convention in this period that the archbishoprics of Armagh and Dublin were reserved to Englishmen, and that mere Irishmen could aspire no higher than the archbishoprics of Cashel and Tuam. This, at any rate, was the explanation, or rather excuse, offered to Agar and his backers when Robinson's candidate, Robert Fowler, bishop of Killaloe, an Englishman, was leap-frogged over Agar to Dublin. Fowler had been bishop of Killaloe only since 1771, and therefore was somewhat junior to Agar in seniority as a bishop; Killaloe was a junior bishopric to Cloyne; and Fowler, a 'paltry, pragmatical man of straw' (according to an Agar partisan), in no way came up to Scott's résumé of Agar as 'infinitely the first ecclesiastic' in the House of Lords. It may be suspected that Robinson wanted not only to keep Agar out, but to put in someone who would constitute no threat to Robinson. The 'reserved to Englishmen' rule had not been invariably applied to the archbishopric of Dublin: even since the death of William King in 1729, one incumbent, Arthur Smyth, archbishop, 1766–71, had been Irish. If ever there was an occasion to set the rule aside, it was the present, not only because of Agar's infinite superiority to Fowler, but because Agar was well connected in British government circles and 'strongly attached to England'.[74]

Robinson's influence in British government circles was, however, to

prove stronger than Agar's on this occasion. This principally consisted of Robinson's old friendship with Lord George Sackville/Germain,
whose secretaryship of state for the colonies was at this time, because
of the American War, the key Cabinet office. As John Scott wrote
pithily to Agar: 'The Primate and Lord G.G. have damned you'. The
incompetent Buckinghamshire, who rightly regarded Germain as his
only friend in the Cabinet, also assisted in damning Agar;
Buckinghamshire knew that his position was under threat because of
the representations to Lord North made by 'a paltry faction inimical
to me', one of whom was Agar. Buckinghamshire ought in fact to
have been removed. But he was reprieved by the characteristic inertia
of North, who on this occasion had the good excuse that it would be
extraordinarily difficult to find anyone willing to succeed
Buckinghamshire at such a difficult time. In early December 1778, a
still-optimistic Agarite mole in Dublin Castle thought that 'the
Fowler' had 'overshot his mark'. It was actually Agar and Welbore
Ellis who had overshot theirs. They had turned the filling of an Irish
archbishopric – not normally a matter of very serious concern unless
it was Armagh – into an issue of confidence in the lord lieutenant and
a source of division within the British Cabinet in the middle of a
world war. As Robinson smugly reassured Chief Secretary Heron in
mid-December, on the eve of the denouement, 'The English Ministry
have sometimes interposed when they wished to promote a Bishop
from the English Bench, but in cases of translations, the Lord
Lieutenant has always been understood as the sole judge ... The
Bishop of Cloyne's friends in England will soon see that the Lord
Lieutenant's recommendation must finally prevail.' It had also been a
tactical error on the part of 'the Bishop of Cloyne's friends in
England' to have taken up the cause of Hely-Hutchinson with the
British government. This had caused Robinson to appeal to Germain,
and had given Robinson the chance to bring what Scott called his
'Machiavellian cunning and hypocrisy' to bear on the filling of the
archbishopric. The primate had actually no formal role, even a con-
sultative one, in Irish episcopal appointments; his influence over such
things varied from primate to primate and according to the circumstances of the time. In the circumstances of late 1778,
Buckinghamshire and Germain were only too happy to have the

authority of Robinson's ecclesiastical office to back their purely political decision.

After Dublin had been filled to Robinson's liking in December 1778, his self-confidence as a politician soared and carried him far 'out of the line of my profession'. It was reported in April 1779 that 'The Primate has a very high opinion of Mr [Thomas] Kelly's fitness in all respects for the office of Solicitor-General'. In light of subsequent events, it looks as if Robinson was grooming Kelly as a rival to Agar's friend and ally, John Scott. Later in the year Robinson, in response to soundings from Lord Hillsborough, declared himself 'entirely for' the latter's pet project of a Union. But this period of political resurgence was short-lived. Implacable in his jealousy and hatred of Agar, Robinson had warned Buckinghamshire that 'a promise of Cashel ... will give a security that may prove inconvenient to the Lord Lieutenant'. But Buckinghamshire did not dare to act on this advice and had given Agar more than a half-promise. When the Archbishop of Cashel died in August 1779, Agar was appointed to succeed him.

ROBINSON'S ECLIPSE
1780–86

WITH AGAR'S PROMOTION to Cashel against Robinson's wishes and intrigues, the predictions that Robinson would be eclipsed by Agar in both ability and influence were fulfilled. However, Robinson continued to practise 'Machiavellian cunning and hypocrisy'. Writing to congratulate Agar (!) in mid-August 1779, Robinson observed that Agar would have 'employment which will not be disagreeable to a man actuated by such clear ideas of order and regularity as you had manifested in the diocese you have left'.[75] In July 1780, he wrote from England to thank Agar for the 'account you give me of your employment in the [Irish Privy] Council … My attention has been employed in the same manner for some years without a coadjutor.'[76] If Agar had been such an efficient bishop, and Robinson in such need of a 'coadjutor', why was it that Robinson had blocked Agar's promotion at every turn and by every means, and had sponsored the mediocre Fowler?

Robinson had guaranteed in December 1778 that Fowler would live up to Robinson's recommendation: 'his character in all respects is unexceptionable, and in my opinion his public conduct will be always clear and consistent'. If this was Robinson's sincere opinion, which is unlikely, it was a sad reflection on his judgement, and it certainly did not survive a 'dispute … conducted with great heat' between them in 1783–4 over their relative precedence in the newly constituted Order of St Patrick. Under the statutes of the Order, the archbishop of Dublin was to be its chancellor – a natural arrangement, 'since the headquarters of the Order lay within his province'. But Robinson

23

seems to have 'expressed his strong indignation at such an appointment, and pressed his own claims as holder of the senior archbishopric, not only to a position in the Order, but also to one superior to
that held by the archbishop of Dublin'. He was pacified by the 3rd
Earl Temple, the lord lieutenant who founded the Order, with a hasti-
ly dreamt-up office of 'prelate'. It was now Fowler's turn to be 'outra-
geous about the Primate's prelacy', and the matter was still simmering
a year later when Temple's successor, the 4th Duke of Rutland, wrote:

> A dispute has arisen between the Primate and the Archbishop of
> Dublin with respect to the precedence on the ceremonial of the
> Order of St Patrick. The Primate claims to walk single. The
> Archbishop claims to walk at the Primate's left hand. I ask for your
> [Temple's] opinion and decision as to what was understood and
> intended as to their particular ranks when you founded the Order.
> The matter seems trifling but the dispute is conducted with great
> heat.

The newly-appointed prelate was also assigned the chancellor's former
duty of administering the oath of new knights at their investiture.[77]

Relations between Robinson and Fowler continued to deteriorate,
and, in the end, even Robinson was sickened by the time-serving way
in which Fowler was to put self-interest ahead of the interests of the
Church. In May 1788, he admitted to Agar his dismay (and this was
tough talking by Robinson's standards) 'that we cannot much depend
on the natural and principal resources [Fowler] in difficulties such as
exist at present'.[78] Actually, the same could have been said of
Robinson himself in 1778, when he too had put self-interest ahead of
the interests of the Church on the issue of Catholic Relief.

From 1780, it was clear that Agar was not so much Robinson's
'coadjutor' as his successor in the leadership of the Church. At the
beginning of February 1780, when the bishops were mustering their
forces for a last (and unavailing) effort to defeat the second attempt
at repealing the Test (19 & 20 Geo. III, c. 6), it was Agar who led
them (and tried to put some fight into Robinson). In a letter intended to be seen by Lord North, he wrote:

> I waited upon the Primate (who I knew to be an enemy upon prin-
> ciple to this bill), [and] stated to him the fatal consequences which

seemed likely to me to arise out of it to this kingdom and the obvious embarrassment which it must occasion to the King's affairs in England [where the dissenters had for some time been agitating for the same relaxation]. I must here do his Grace the justice to say that his ardour to prevent the evil effects ... to this country did not exceed his anxious efforts to relieve English administration ... We therefore determined to try whether we could not prevail on the Bishops now in Dublin to apply by a joint letter to the Archbishop of Canterbury to use his endeavours in the Privy Council of England to suppress the bill, if that be possible; but, should he fail in that, to have it altered by the addition to the end of the Bill of a clause which substitutes a declaration to be made by every person in lieu of the Sacramental Test.[79]

On 2 May, Agar, the archbishop of Tuam and two bishops (one of them Robinson's old antagonist, Charles Jackson) – alone among the members of the House of Lords – recorded themselves as 'dissentient' when the bill passed the Lords, and Agar also entered a solitary, more strongly worded protest.[80] Robinson held back. In July 1780, on the question of the Tenantry Bill (a measure which, among other things, would minimise the possibility of recovering alienated church lands), Robinson – then absent in England – wrote to Agar to 'express my concern when I perceive that the temper of the rising generation in the House of Commons is equally hostile to the rights of the clergy as I have ever found it'.[81] On 19 August, the opposition to the bill in the Lords, headed by Agar, was defeated by only one vote. On the same day, a dissentient minority of twenty-one lords entered a protest in the Lords' *Journals*. In this protest, and in another of 3 May 1782 against the 'Act to permit Marriages by Dissenting Teachers', Robinson took precedence over him, but Agar's papers again show that Agar had taken the lead by drafting the protests.[82] On the issue of the contemporary Catholic Relief Acts, which the bishops modified but did not oppose *in limine*, Agar was reported by the conservative catholic leader, the 4th Viscount Kenmare, to be pressing on Robinson a plan for 'the nomination to vacant catholic sees [to be] vested in the Crown', and to be stimulating him and others to successful opposition to the Catholic Education Bill, as originally drafted.[83]

Robinson's renunciation of his leadership role as primate – in fact, his cession of it to Agar – certainly did not derive from any spirit of toleration. His attitude to the Irish catholics – notwithstanding the 'liberal and temperate' sentiments he had professed in 1778 – actually became increasingly hardline. In January 1765, it had been alleged – very fancifully – that his appointment was 'highly acceptable by the commonality who, being mostly Roman Catholics, naturally preferred the moderate principles of an Englishman to the early Protestant bigotry a Scotchman or an Irishman imbibes'.[84] He had not exhibited these 'moderate principles' in his one surviving sermon, preached in 1757 to both Houses of Parliament on the anniversary of the 1641 rising. This was routinely the occasion for expressions of protestant triumphalism, but Robinson went beyond the common form when he denounced 'the papal superstition' and 'the stupendous fabric of papal tyranny'.[85] Over the years, these sentiments hardened into something approaching alarmist extremism. From the early 1780s, he spent an increasing amount of time, and from 1786 all of his time, in retreat in England, spreading more gloom and despondency than even the Irish situation merited – or, as John Scott put it in 1784, 'croaking all manner of discontent'.[86] At about the same time, the then lord lieutenant, Rutland (who was himself fairly inventive of popish plots), remarked impatiently: 'The Primate, with the utmost zeal for the good of the two kingdoms, is too apt to despond; [and] his prejudices against the Roman Catholics increase his apprehensions'.[87] The hostile reaction of British Ministers to Robinson's 'croaking' was stronger. In the years when the policy of Catholic Relief gathered momentum in British governmental circles, the views of the Primate of All Ireland on the subject could, with a facility dangerous to the Church, be dismissed as those of a crank.

ROBINSON'S MISSING YEARS

1786–94[88]

R OBINSON'S CHOICE OF FOWLER as his second-in-command came to matter very much after he himself left Ireland – as things turned out, never to return – in October 1786. His departure, which Agar almost 'prevailed to prevent',[89] could not have been worse timed. The period 1785–8 was that of the Rightboy disturbances, which were directed with great violence and intimidation against the collection of tithes, and against all concerned in it, in Agar's province of Munster. The government's response included some mild and vague proposals of 1786 for the improvement of clerical performance and the reform of the tithe system, and a number of substantive and more sweeping proposals of the same nature initiated or countenanced in 1788 by the patronising and overbearing Lord Buckingham (formerly Lord Temple), lord lieutenant for the second time, 1787–9. Robinson's absence, his quarrel with Fowler and his jealousy of and uneasy relations with Agar, told against united episcopal action; and Fowler, predictably, proved a malleable instrument in the hands of a forceful lord lieutenant, as Buckingham proved to be. This meant that the role of champion of the interests of the Church of Ireland devolved on Agar. Writing later and in another context, an admirer of Agar remarked that 'the Rock of Cashel was not to be moved'. However, not even 'the Rock of Cashel' could stand without the support of Robinson, because of Robinson's rank and authority and the independence of government which they gave him, and because of the impossibility of looking for support to Fowler. Everything in Agar's correspondence, and not just in his letters to

Robinson, suggests that he was scrupulous in giving Robinson his place as primate, looked to Robinson for the exercise of his primatial authority, and only became highly irritated when Robinson failed to give directions or assistance to those on the spot.

From the letters which Robinson wrote to Agar from Bath during 1787, it soon became clear how much help Robinson was going to be in a situation which he admitted was 'alarming'. In late January, he declined to be involved in the drafting of measures to compensate the clergy for their losses of tithe income in 1786 and to restore order in Munster, making the excuse 'that my opinion might be misapprehended and of course not truly represented', and that the matter should be 'left ... to the wisdom and prudence of government'.[90] Accordingly, the Clergy Compensation, the Whiteboy and the Magistracy Acts were passed with a considerable contribution from Agar and none from Robinson. In December, Agar submitted to him a proposal of Agar's that the purposes of the parliamentary grant to the Board of First Fruits should be broadened into the buying of glebes and the building of glebe-houses, in addition to the building of churches. Robinson rejected this proposal for 'prudential reasons' (and in 1789 Agar, ignoring these, went ahead without him). For present purposes, what is important is Robinson's concluding remark: 'This is my decided opinion ... But I mention it to *you* only at present, as I shall not interpose in the business unless I find it necessary to give my opinion.' This of course was a subject on which the Primate of All Ireland's opinion should *not* have been a secret; nor should such an important initiative have had to come from the archbishop who was only third in seniority within the Church of Ireland. In mid-January 1788, Buckingham unfolded to Agar, and Agar immediately reported to Robinson, Buckingham's ideas for 'hostile, indigested innovations' (as Robinson called them) in the governance of the Church of Ireland. These principally comprised legislation to enforce clerical residence by means other than episcopal authority, and to impose financial and other burdens on the clergy – thereby, as Agar saw it, giving the countenance of the government to propagandist claims that the greed and negligence of the clergy had caused the Rightboy disturbances. Though unprepared for Buckingham's specific arguments and proposals, Agar countered them firmly and effectively in the audience to which he was summoned. Robinson, however – instead of praising Agar's political courage – actually had the nerve to suggest that Agar should have said more! 'It would not have been improper, before you quitted the room, if you had desired him to inform you what were the measures he proposed to adopt to check the violent and oppressive spirit which is the evil of the present hour and which [?threatneth] the being of the Established Church.'

In spite of the crass insensitivity of this remark, and the contrast between the course which Robinson recommended to Agar and that which he pursued himself, Agar continued to seek guidance from Robinson. One of the next issues to be discussed was a request from the chief secretary's office to each diocesan for a return of the state of his diocese in regard to clerical residence. Responding to Agar's call for leadership and action, Robinson wrote at the end of January 1788: 'I have strong objections to a compliance with this article ... But, as I am absent, I believe I shall do nothing, unless upon a fresh application. Was I in Dublin, I would frame such a return as I understood would be satisfactory to the L[ord] L[ieutenant] and deliver it to him.' Events then moved too fast for reference to Robinson to be possible. Two separate bills were introduced, one after the other, into the House of Commons – the first fixing the tithe on hemp at 5s. per acre (and threatening a similar modus on flax and other items), and the second exempting from tithe for seven years 'barren lands' which were in the process of being improved. Agar, who had agreed to accept the first bill if it were confined to hemp and were couched in such terms as precluded its being used as a precedent for other commutations, was eventually successful in persuading Buckingham to adhere to this compromise. On the second bill, however, over which there had been no previous negotiation between the bishops and the Castle, and which was brought forward by Henry Grattan without warning, Agar led a successful opposition in the House of Lords. He carried an amendment giving to the ecclesiastical courts sole jurisdiction in disputes over what constituted barrenness and improvement. This was, in effect, a wrecking amendment, and the Commons sulkily dropped the bill on its return to that House.

Writing to Welbore Ellis in mid-April, Agar expressed his

serious apprehensions for what may happen in another session of parliament. The Primate's absence and the part which the Archbishop of
D[ublin] has taken in all these matters, together with the desertion
of two or three more of the b[isho]ps [William Beresford and
Richard Marlay], must give our enemies such encouragement as cannot fail to produce various attempts to invade the property of the
Church. Hitherto, we have, I thank God, defended ourselves, though
with great difficulty. But to me it seems very doubtful how long we
may be able to do so.

His 'serious apprehensions' were well founded. Buckingham reacted
to the modification or loss of the bills by pressing on with prepara-
tions for the Clerical Residence Bill which he had already adumbrat-
ed to Agar and which he intended to introduce in the next session of
parliament. Robinson acknowledged that this 'critical situation of …
affairs in Ireland requires my fullest exertions', but pleaded that he
was 'disabled from undertaking a journey to Ireland and am directed
to return to the hot wells at Bristol'. He advised Agar to prepare two
forestalling measures, a Barren Lands Bill containing proper safe-
guards for tithes, and a bill to regulate Faculties (i.e. restrain non-res-
idence), and seek to obtain Buckingham's approbation of them before
worse befell. 'If this is not done by the bishops, some hard bill and
oppressive to the clergy will probably receive the assent of both
Houses.' Agar was opposed in principle to the second, because he
believed strongly that the regulation of the clergy was a matter for the
episcopate, not parliament. But he agreed in principle with the first –
though he did not in fact sponsor a Barren Lands Bill until 1793 (33
Geo. III, c. 25), under the safer auspices of Buckingham's successor.
In the spring of 1788, as on other occasions, Robinson showed that,
even in his old age, he was a flexible and resourceful political tacti-
cian. However, he declined to take a lead and make himself unpopu-
lar in any influential quarter.

To what extent his illness was genuine, and to what extent assumed,
is hard to establish. A myth has gained currency that he had been seriously ill in 1769. But this is based on a misreading by Sir John Gilbert
of the date of a letter which he published in 1881 in an Historical
Manuscripts Commission *Report*: the illness referred to was in fact the
last illness of Primate Stone in December *1764*. The 'regimen', 'diet'

and course of 'physic' attributed to Robinson in the early 1770s by Richard Cumberland, which included numerous 'rhubarb pills' and fighting off 'the bile with raw eggs and mutton broth mixed up with muscovado sugar', suggest that he was a hypochondriac. Robinson may have taken after his elder brother, William, who succeeded to the family baronetcy in 1777 and whom Cumberland described as 'a feeble, infirm man and a real valetudinarian'. In October 1785, Robinson's fellow-Yorkshireman, John Hotham, bishop of Clogher, feared the effects on Robinson of the death of 'Sir William Robinson ... [his] only surviving brother. This, from the extreme regard subsisting all their lives between them, I fear will shock *my friend* fundamentally ... [who may] droop and exchange this life for a better.' Others took Robinson's drooping state less seriously. John Scott, alluding to Agar's ambition for the primacy, had quipped in May 1783 that the 74-year-old Robinson was 'a very tough incumbent, in fine preservation';[91] and it was noteworthy that, in the years of Robinson's absence from Ireland, he always 'kept a hospitable table'. In late November 1786, Chief Secretary Orde, who had 'had much conversation ... to no great purpose' with Robinson in Bath during Robinson's first weeks away from Ireland, saw no reason why Robinson should not return to London for a discussion with the Prime Minister, Pitt, on the Rightboys and Church reform, and then to Ireland to do his duty there. Rutland felt the same, and Pitt intended to 'make a point of it'. All three were, of course, to be disappointed.

Thereafter, the major source of information about Robinson's health is Welbore Ellis's letters to Agar which, since Ellis was himself inclined to be a *malade imaginaire*, ought perhaps to be taken at a discount. In mid-May 1787, Ellis wrote: 'I am very sorry to understand that my old friend, the Primate, has had an unpleasant attack of either gravel or stone. This is indeed a lamentable event, as it will make the reminder of his life probably very painful, and he has been induced to try a quack medicine which has made his case worse. He is, as I am informed, at present at Clifton, near Bristol Wells.' In March 1788, Robinson returned to London, 'as I understand, in good health', and in early May he was 'still in London, well in health, but has not as yet fixed any time for his departure'. By late May, however, he was 'firmly convinced of the impossibility of performing the journey [to Ireland]. To say the truth, he is much altered ..., is grown pale and languid, can't bear going about the streets in a carriage, declines very much the dining from home, and when in company has not his usual spirits.' Then, in late August:

> The reason he [Robinson] alleges why he cannot go to Ireland, though he might reach Holyhead by easy journeys, is that the sea always brought on convulsive spasms, and he is fully persuaded that it would now revive those dreadful spasms in his bladder, which he thinks of with horror. Besides, whether he moves from Bristol to London or back again, he never is far from skilful advice and assistance, if he should be stopped on the road by one of the paroxysms of his complaint, but if that happened in Wales he thinks he might perish in tortures. But the less able he may think himself for going there, the more strongly is he called upon for exerting himself *here*, where I think he might do most essential service.

Genuine or otherwise, Robinson's illness clearly had to be accepted as an accomplished fact; and from this point on, as the last sentence of Ellis's letter suggests, Agar and Ellis concentrated on ways of limiting the damage being done by Robinson's absence. While Ellis tried to prevail on him to render 'essential service' by speaking to Pitt and/or the King, Agar continued to urge him to write to Buckingham or to make some public declaration for Irish consumption. Agar argued at the beginning of June:

> I entirely agree with your Grace that, if a proper [Barren Lands] Bill of this kind ... should be drawn and submitted to the Lord Lieutenant, it would probably be accepted and supported, and prevent many crude and improper plans from being obtruded upon us ... [But] why should you not *yourself* transmit it to his Excellency for his consideration? He would probably accept such a bill coming from *you* and to be supported by your brethren, much rather than hazard the success of one not sanctioned by such authority.

Robinson talked big about a Barren Lands Bill: referring in July 1788 to the previous bill which Agar had succeeded in fatally amending, he boasted (again with crass insensitivity) that 'if *he* had been on the spot, he should not have attempted to have only amended or qualified it, but would have opposed it directly and done his utmost to have it thrown out'. But he was not prepared to take any one decisive step in the matter. To Ellis, he reported that

> he had two long conferences with his brother of L[ambe]th, who … suggested, after he had perused the *circular* and plan of reform whether, as [the] P[rimate]'s health would not permit him to go over, he would not do the next-best service in his power by explaining fully to the M[inister, Pitt] the importance of the subject and prevent him from being misled by other representations and induced to adopt measures from which it might be difficult to recede. [The] P[rimate] replied that *he* had a great difficulty in his way, for hitherto the L[ord] L[ieutenant] had acted towards him with the appearance of some confidence and of some consideration, which he should endeavour to make use of to dissuade or divert him from the most objectionable parts of his plan … but …, if he should go to the M[inister, who was Buckingham's cousin] …, he should lose all means of doing good in one quarter and perhaps in both.

Ellis subsequently ascertained from Archbishop Moore of Canterbury that the latter did not agree with Robinson in this delicacy.

At this point Agar lost his temper, and wrote Robinson a letter which began with the following (by late eighteenth-century standards) strong language:

> To the three last letters which I wrote to your Grace I have not had the honour of receiving any answer: a circumstance which would certainly prevent me from troubling you again on any subject but that of the Church of Ireland, over which your Grace presides and which in the first instance is committed to your care. Personal respect for your Grace and for your station has hitherto determined me to solicit your opinion on all matters of importance, and not to commit myself in any measure of consequence to the welfare or government of the Church without first knowing your sentiments … I wish much to know your Grace's final opinion on this subject, that I may regulate my conduct accordingly, on which probably that of some others may depend.

Robinson replied huffily: 'My means of information in every respect, particularly as to the temper of the Castle, in my present situation, [were] very imperfect … If you cannot make allowance for these and many other similar circumstances arising from my absence and the fluctuating state of my health, our correspondence will no longer be confidential or satisfactory to either of us.' He persisted in his already exploded view that it was better for the Church that he preserve his flimsy relationship with Buckingham and communicate privately with the latter to the exclusion of the rest of the bishops. Agar, perforce, had to content himself with this final evasion. He continued to correspond with Robinson over tactics and measures for the next session of parliament, and even wrote to him at the end of October:

> As I have reason to suspect that much pains have been taken [by Buckingham] to misrepresent my conduct where I most wish to have it rightly understood [in the eyes of the king], I place a full confidence in your Grace's wisdom and justice ... for a fair and impartial statement of my conduct ... [which] has been productive of many serious inconveniences to me, which I might have escaped as easily as others, had I been equally indifferent to the true interests of the Church of Ireland.

But it is unlikely that Agar expected Robinson to do anything of the sort: rather, the passage must surely be interpreted as implying that Robinson was one of those who had 'escaped ... many serious inconveniences' through being 'indifferent to the true interests of the Church of Ireland'.

The danger to the Church in the next session of parliament which Agar had foretold, and to which Robinson's pusillanimity materially contributed, evaporated for the time being because of the Regency Crisis of 1788–9. Between 1790 and 1794 (the year of Robinson's death), the danger took a new form. Now it was the British government's Catholic Relief measures, first enacted for Britain in 1791 and then, more radically, for Ireland in 1792–3. A letter to Agar of early February 1792 about the Catholic Relief Bill of that year shows that Robinson was still up to his old tricks. The writer was Richard Woodward, Agar's successor (bar one short-lived, intervening incumbent) as bishop of Cloyne, who was at Bath at the same time as Robinson:

> The moment is an awful one, beyond any I ever saw ... I urged [on Robinson], as far as I could with propriety, the great importance that

it would be of … that his opinions, expressed to me repeatedly, should be known in Ireland. I even went so far as to urge that he would authorise some person to declare them, as *commissioned* by him. This he declined, as not wishing to assume so much, but said that he thought, *and did not desire to keep his opinion secret*, that the [proposed] *concessions to the Roman Catholics … would endanger the Protestant interest in Ireland.* Being determined to know how far I had his permission to go, I asked whether I was at liberty to mention so much to a friend by letter. He said I was at liberty. The best use I can make of this liberty is to inform your Grace.

To his son-in-law, Woodward wrote more freely. 'The Primate croaks if possible more than I do.' 'I have sent my proxy to the Archbishop of Cashel, on whom I depend for a strenuous opposition to it [the bill]. The Primate thinks it will have been thrown out.' In other words, Robinson 'croaked' but was not prepared to do anything except hope for the best. By September 1792, both Woodward and he feared that there would be disturbances in Ireland and consequent non-payment of rent, and the public-spirited resolution which both adopted was to instruct their respective agents to send over to Bath as much spare cash as possible.

ROBINSON AS BUILDER
AND BENEFACTOR
1765–94

———◆———

ROBINSON'S POLITICAL RECORD, and in particular the quality of his political leadership of the Church, have not hitherto been much examined because he has been regarded as an apolitical, 'enlightened and beneficent' primate,[92] whose importance lies in his buildings and benefactions. Over time, these buildings and benefactions have assumed almost legendary proportions; so it is time that they were subjected to some re-examination. The first, simple point to be made about them is that they, too, were heavily concentrated on Robinson's first and best twelve years.

Immediately on his promotion to Armagh in 1765, he turned his attention to the long-neglected music of the cathedral.[93] Although the existing organ had been 'repaired twice in the 1750s', in other respects there had been musical stagnation since the death of Primate Lindsay in 1724. In particular, Primate Stone had compounded his own absenteeism by 'giving vicar choralships in Armagh to men resident in Dublin'. Robinson already owned 'a small, seven-stop, portable chest organ built ... in 1742' by John Snetzler (1710–85), a Swiss who had settled in London c.1740 and 'was very much the leading [organ] builder of the day'. Accordingly, in 1765, Robinson commissioned from Snetzler and presented to the cathedral 'a new organ possessed of many stops and of most pleasing and powerful tones'. The existing organ was retained, apparently for choir practice, and the new one installed in a loft or gallery (and subsequently moved about in the wake of Robinson's attempts to add a new tower to the cathedral). There already was one full-scale Snetzler organ in Ireland, in the Rotunda rooms, Dublin, and a couple more were to follow as a result of Robinson's trend-setting (including Lord Hillsborough's in Hillsborough parish church, Co. Down). But the late nineteenth-century architect and organ buff, Sir Thomas Drew, pronounced the Armagh instrument 'Snetzler's finest Irish organ'. Nor, in fairness to Robinson, is this to be ascribed to mere self-gratification. Robinson held that music had a serious pastoral purpose, as is shown by 'his forthright advice to a clergyman concerned to recover his dissenting parishioners: "If you wish to get these people back again, sing them in. They won't come to your preaching; argument will do nothing with them; but they have itching ears and will listen to a hymn."'[94]

Robinson also attended almost immediately to the fabric of the cathedral. He

> appropriated a considerable sum towards the task and … this was further augmented by subscriptions from the dean and chapter. Stuart[95] says that the Dean and each member of the chapter 'subscribed, we believe, £50, about the 28th of August 1766 …'. When … Robinson had collected his funds, he began his improvements on the cathedral by slating the western aisle which had been previously shingled by Margetson [archbishop, 1663–78] … [and fitting] the interior in a manner which he considered more suitable for divine service.[96]

Chart expresses some misgivings about these 'improvements'. 'He repaired and, in the view of that time, embellished his cathedral … but with little sympathy for its original characteristics. Most unfortunately, he removed the [c.1613–25?] tracery of the west windows and replaced it by a commonplace, modern window opening.'[97] This echoes the earlier doubts of Edward Rogers, deputy keeper of the Robinson Library in Armagh (1838–94), who in his *Topographical Sketches of Armagh and Tyrone* (Armagh, 1874) lamented that 'the liberality and munificence of Primate Robinson was not guided by good taste or by any respect for the ancient remains of the country to which he had been removed. When Bishop of Ferns, he had part of the venerable old cathedral pulled down in order to build the walls of the churchyard, and he surrounded the walls of the ancient abbey of Armagh with the farm offices' for the new palace which he built on his demesne land on the outskirts of the city.

Following his initial building work on the cathedral in the mid-1760s, Robinson in 1782–3 made a famous attempt to replace the existing tower with a 100-foot one 'in imitation of that of Magdalen College, Oxford'. In spite of the best endeavours of his architect, Thomas Cooley (1740–84), to support the structure with strengthened internal arches and additional external buttresses, the new tower caused a panic among the local anglicans

> that the entire fabric would tumble and bury the congregation in its ruins. ... Robinson then [1783] ordered the new tower to be pulled down, even to the roof of the building from whence it sprang, that is, to the very spot from which the old one, carrying its spire, cross and weather-cock had been removed. Thus ended the Magdalen steeple. In the year 1784 ... Cooley died and [his Armagh-born pupil] Francis Johnston [1760–1829] became architect to His Grace, and by his express directions made a plan as near as possible to that of the original steeple, with the exception of having two windows, on each side of the tower, instead of one. This plan, Mr Johnston put into execution by raising the tower on the old piers and arches, about 38 feet above the roof of the church to the top of the battlements with a spire of about 40 feet more.

However, even this last and least ambitious spire had eventually to be taken down.[98] Thereafter, the cathedral remained untouched until the primacy of Lord John George Beresford, who between the years 1834 and 1840 is estimated to have spent £34,463 18s. 7 3/4d. on repairs (£24,000 of which was donated by the Primate himself).'[99] So, Robinson's 'restoration' of the cathedral was costly (and not just to him), controversial and counter-productive.

Chart, apart from his already-quoted strictures on Robinson's disregard for 'original characteristics', was enthusiastic (in one or two respects – as will be seen – unduly so) about

> the princely benefactions in which he delighted. It is no exaggeration to say that he transformed his primatial city of Armagh, which ... became a city of stone dwellings, its many hills crowned with stately public buildings. Robinson ... inserted in leases of see property a condition requiring that any building erected should be of a substantial type ... [He] was a bachelor and devoted his savings to his

projects ... He built a palace for himself, commodious and impressive ... [On Vicar's Hill, he] built beside ... [the cathedral] houses for its officers reproducing something of that effect of seclusion and peace which their closes give to some English cathedrals. He was the chief mover in the erection of a public infirmary and barracks [1773–4]. He built and endowed a public school [1774], an excellent library [1771] (containing even now the finest collection of manuscripts and rare books to be found in Ireland outside Dublin), and somewhat of a novelty in the country, an observatory [1789–91]. It was his ambition, never realised, to make Armagh the centre of a university for the north of Ireland, and certainly he had provided beforehand several of the institutions that it would have required.[100]

Constantia Maxwell echoed these sentiments – minus the criticism of Robinson's lack of respect for earlier architecture. Other commentators, however, have drawn attention to the essential modesty – not to say economy – of his buildings. In 1778, the Rev. John Wesley described the new palace as 'neat and handsome, but not magnificent'.[101] In recent years, Dr Neely has pointed out that Robinson's buildings were less ambitious than is suggested by the inscriptions over the entrances to two of them – the library ('The medicine shop of the soul'), and the observatory ('The heavens declare the glory of God').

> He was both a man of taste and caution. He built well, but not extravagantly ... The palace was a comparatively small building; so much so that Lord John George Beresford [archbishop of Armagh, 1822–62, unfortunately] ... felt constrained to ... add a third storey ... [Robinson's] architects ... Cooley and ... Johnston, designed in a pure and simple classical style. The library, above all, is a monument of elegance and restraint.[102]

In the view of Dr Edward McParland, Robinson's buildings were not only restrained but 'dull' – an adjective which has been applied to Robinson himself. Robinson, writes McParland, 'provided buildings for the practical purposes of worship. [He] neither invoked ([n]or was alert to) the symbolical value of great architecture ... [He] frustrated Thomas Cooley's brilliant potential by feeding him fat commissions for dull buildings.'[103]

To her otherwise laudatory description of Robinson and all his works, Constantia Maxwell added the rider that he was ostentatious and over-fond of veneration. This was the recorded view of at least one contemporary, the already-mentioned John Hotham. Hotham, then a viceregal chaplain, was taken under Robinson's wing (perhaps because Hotham was the brother-in-law of the Lord Lieutenant, Buckinghamshire), and invited to Armagh in October 1778. Reporting on this visit in a letter to his elder brother in London, Hotham pointed out that Robinson could well afford to be generous, and that his generosity was more than tinged with vanity:

> I must insist (if you please) on finishing my career with the primacy, the income being only between £8,000 and £9,000 per annum at present. I am just [October 1778] returned from Armagh, which is indeed a magnificent thing, and will be more and more so every year … The Primate is going to England, and after he has used the Bath waters awhile, means to pass most of the winter in London. As soon as you meet him there, 'if you value your life, this remember to do': take your watch in your hand and flatter him in my name by the hour about his creations at Armagh, his munificence, magnificence, noble public-spiritedness, foresight, taste, wisdom and astonishing success as to improvements, in so short a term of years. You may safely do so, for he really deserves it all; and as it is his hobby-horse, he will bite like any gudgeon. I am not holding him cheap in what I say, for upon my honour I think him by very far the greatest man in this country, though he does not like women so well as you and I have formerly done.[104]

Others, too, played on Robinson's vanity. In 1784, the master of Drogheda school wrote to him: 'I fear for the roof of this house, unless repaired immediately … [but] I am afraid to do it at my own expense … Your Grace is the father of schools, and of this in particular. I have therefore made bold to trouble you with the enclosed account and to beg your protection.'[105] More dangerously, Buckingham tried in 1788 to soften Robinson's reaction to his '*circular* and plan of [Church] reform' by prefacing them with a laudatory reference to Robinson's 'piety and discretion'.[106] Ironically, in view of Robinson's reputation for biting 'like any gudgeon', Stuart described him as 'inaccessible to flatterers'.[107]

Two years before Hotham's letter, an arch-flatterer of Robinson's 'creations at Armagh', Arthur Young, had written his famous account of them, which was soon to be published. Entertained and patronised by the Primate (who was careful to subscribe for three copies of Young's forthcoming book), the impressionable and very commercial Young puffed Robinson's 'creations at Armagh' exactly to Robinson's own specification. Thus was born, among other things, the legend that, before the coming of Robinson, Armagh consisted of 'a nest of mud cabins' (a favourite term of Young's), and that, following the coming of Robinson, it was 'rising out of its ruins into a large and prosperous city'.[108] The reality was far different. In 1759, it had been described as 'an ugly, scattered town'[109] – which implies size, though certainly not beauty or good layout. In 1760, it had boasted 469 houses, which increased to 482 by 1766 and to 501 by 1770. The 482 houses of 1766 were categorised as: 115 'very good' to 'tolerable' houses; 356 'low' houses to 'ordinary cabins'; and 11 'low cabins', 'waste cabins' or 'ruins'.[110] It is unlikely that any cabins but the lowest were of mud, and clearly there were very few ruins. Long before Robinson, there were a number of well established streets in Armagh with houses built predominantly of coarse rubble stone – Abbey Street, Castle Street, English Street, Irish Street, Jenney's Row, etc. Shortly before Robinson, in 1751–9, there had been a significant exercise in town-planning, which had led to the laying-out of Ogle and Thomas Streets. Even in Vicar's Hill, the terrace alongside the cathedral mainly built by Robinson in 1776–80, the four best houses date from 1724.[111]

In other respects, too, Robinson's personal role in the development of his archiepiscopal capital has been unduly magnified. First, though he encouraged the building boom in Armagh which began soon after he became primate, the boom was based broadly on economic prosperity (the fact that the city had the biggest brown linen market in Ulster in the period c.1770–c.1820), not narrowly on Robinson's patronage.[112] Second, Robinson controlled the Armagh corporation and its revenues and was the ground landlord of Armagh; this placed him – in comparison to other bishops and indeed lay landlords – in an unusual and very favourable position of local monopoly.[113] Third, the diocese of Armagh had a higher parochial and glebe income in 1765, and was more amply endowed with churches and glebe-houses, than any other diocese in Ireland, which meant that Robinson was relatively free to concentrate his resources on his cathedral city (not that he neglected the rest of his diocese – the Hon. and Rev. William Stuart, archbishop of Armagh, 1800–22, found that the residence record of the clergy of Armagh was 'as perfect as any English diocese with which I am acquainted'[114]). Finally, Robinson's resources, in annual rental income, fees, proxies, etc., were at least double those of every other bishop of the Church of Ireland, except the undeserving Earl-Bishop of Derry, and three or four times the size of the incomes of most of them. In other words, Robinson was uniquely placed to be 'princely' in his 'benefactions'. From him to whom much had been given, much was to be expected, or – as John Wesley deflatingly put it – 'So much good may any man of a large fortune do, if he lays it out to the best advantage'.[115]

Furthermore, Robinson's already-mentioned palace in Armagh, the most impressive of his 'creations', turns out not to have been a benefaction at all. Dr Hotham, the viceregal chaplain on the make, had been disconcerted by all the expenses attending promotion to an Irish bishopric, and particularly attending the episcopal palace. However, he reported that during his visit to Armagh, Robinson had

> set my mind considerably at ease with regard to the raising and recovering of the sums necessary to be paid on coming to a see or on building a new house, if there should be none upon it. The matter, as he has explained it, is neither difficult, distressing nor cruel, though I had thought it all three. But what signifies this palaver? It is no affair of mine, for not a soul [on the episcopal bench] will go to heaven or anywhere else!

As a result of Robinson's own legislation of 1772 and 1774 (11 & 12 Geo. III, c. 17, s. 3, as explained by 13 & 14 Geo. III, c. 27, s. 6), 'every bishop who built a new house in his see is authorised to charge his immediate successor with the *whole* money so laid out by him, and that whole money is by law allowed to be two full years' income of the bishopric'.[116] Robinson's new palace in Armagh ante-dated this legislation. He had received authority to build it in 1766 and the work was apparently completed (to Cooley's design) by 1770.[117] But much remained to be done to create the palace demesne, and

Robinson did not submit these combined operations for valuation and certification until 1775. This meant that he benefited from his own legislation and that the full cost of his palace and demesne fell upon his successor.

The certificate which he received in December 1775 states that the cost had been £15,081 14s. 5³/4d., that this had been approved by a commission of valuation, and that it did not exceed the clear yearly value of the see over a two-year period (the income of Armagh then being £8,163 17s. 4³/8d. per annum, exclusive of fees and proxies).[118] Not for nothing was it described in 1775 as 'one of the best houses in the kingdom, a real palace suited to his elevated rank'.[119] The £15,000-odd excludes the cost of the nearby archiepiscopal chapel, built c.1781–6 first to the design of Cooley and then, after Cooley's death, to that of Francis Johnston. It is an architectural gem and must have been very costly in relation to its small size. No documentary evidence for the cost seems to have survived, nor does any contemporary or near-contemporary commentator appear to have recorded a good guess. In the absence of such information, it is reasonable to suggest that such a building must have cost something like £3,000. By 1786, the Armagh see rental must have been easily £9,000 a year; so Robinson would have been entitled to charge the full £18,000 (i.e. not more than two years' rental income) on his successor. The only apparently conflicting evidence is the fact that Robinson's successor, 'Primate Newcome ... bound himself to pay to Robinson's heirs a sum of between £15,000 and £16,000'.[120] This might suggest that the chapel cost less than £1,000 (an impossibility) or that it was treated as a separate church and therefore not included in the cost of the palace at all. But it is much more likely to suggest that Newcome made as large a down-payment as he could afford to Robinson's executors, and gave an interest-bearing bond or IOU for the rest.

On this last assumption, Robinson's 'magnificence' must have entailed upon Newcome an expenditure of c.£18,000! (No wonder Newcome 'did nothing to promote'[121] Robinson's last wish, which was for a university to be established in Armagh.) Nor did the consequences of Robinson's acts (in all senses) end there. The legislation of 1772/4 provided that the successor was entitled to recoup three-quarters of his expenditure from the next man in (and so on, by a series of fractions, until the cost was defrayed). When Newcome died in 1800, William Stuart, the second primate after Robinson – faced with what was still a huge bill for the Armagh Palace – tried to evade appointment to the primacy on the ground, among other things, that 'the great expense of taking possession of Armagh would utterly ruin my children'.[122] So, Newcome, Stuart and, in 1822, Primate Beresford paid for Robinson's palace, and the only cost to Robinson was the loss of interest on the sums of money, eventually totalling c.£18,000, spent on the building. This means that what was defining about Robinson's palace-building in Armagh was the simple but extraordinary fact that he was the first primate of modern times to fix Armagh as his official place of residence. Before Robinson, that designation still applied to the long-ruinous archiepiscopal palace at Termonfeckin, outside Drogheda, or to the early seventeenth-century palace in Drogheda itself.[123] His immediate predecessor, Archbishop Stone, had maintained lodgings in English Street, Armagh, suitable for merely temporary periods of residence, and had lived for most of the year – and in 'Polish magnificence'[124] – either in Henrietta Street or in his country retreat in the Dublin area, Leixlip Castle, Co. Kildare. From the outset, Robinson intended to reside more regularly in Armagh, and in grander style than his predecessor. He did not regard Stone's residence in English Street as suitable to the dignity of the primacy; so, while his new palace was being planned and built, he leased nearby Richill from the Richardson family,[125] whose head, William Richardson (1749–1822), was then a minor.

Nevertheless, Robinson maintained other Irish residences besides his successive houses in or near Armagh. He bought from Stone's executors the long-leasehold of Stone's Henrietta Street house in 1765, and leased another country (or, rather, suburban) retreat in the Dublin area, probably in 1769.[126] This was Belvedere, Drumcondra, a small, early eighteenth-century villa which belonged to the Singleton family of Aclare, Co. Meath. Robinson preserved the original panelling (most of which is there to this day), and does not seem to have altered the main block of the house. But it must have been he who added a single-storey (over a basement) extension to the rear, providing a large, handsome reception room with a canted bay. The ceiling is decorated with rococo plasterwork reminiscent of the

1760s, and the add-on might well have been designed by Cooley.[127]

From 1785 onwards, Robinson busied himself in building a new house midway between Dublin and Armagh – Rokeby Hall, Dunleer, Co. Louth. The house is of mixed architectural inspiration. Dr Maurice Craig attributes it to Cooley, who had died before building began, but 'certainly with the participation of Francis Johnston'. Craig also discerns in it the influence of two other houses, Lucan House, Co. Dublin, and Mount Kennedy, Co. Wicklow, and of four other architects, Sir William Chambers, James Wyatt, Michael Stapleton and Richard Johnston. Because of this complex skein, which Craig supposes 'may never be fully unravelled', Rokeby Hall 'is more remarkable for the beauty of its detail than for its overall expression …'.[128] John Wesley, visiting Armagh in June 1787 and recording his admiration of Robinson's demesne and recently completed chapel, expressed amazement that Robinson had abandoned them, and was 'fully taken up in building a large seat near Dublin at above eighty years of age!'.

Wesley seems not to have realised that Robinson was in England and had abandoned Rokeby Hall also; nor was he privy to Robinson's dynastic plans for Rokeby Hall (see below). But he was right to think it remarkable that a man should still be 'taken up in building … at above eighty' (Robinson was actually a mere seventy-eight in 1787). The expression 'taken up in building' is apt. Robinson built, not just in Armagh and for the purpose of making Armagh a primatial capital, but for building's sake. In addition to 'his creations' in Ireland, he spent £6,000 on his former college, Christ Church, Oxford, financing the building of a splendid new quadrangle, gateway and residential block, designed by James Wyatt, begun in 1773 and completed in 1783.[129] Building was in Robinson's blood. His eldest brother, Sir Thomas Robinson, 1st Bt (c.1699–1777), was an uncontrollable amateur architect; and, because he lacked Robinson's resources, Sir Thomas's Palladian rebuilding of the family seat in Yorkshire, Rokeby Park, in the period c.1725–c.1735 had permanently embarrassed his finances.[130]

Robinson's benefactions to Christ Church were small in comparison to his benefactions to Armagh. But even his benefactions to Armagh were smaller than has hitherto been realised. The best source

of information about his buildings, benefactions and will is still
Stuart's *Armagh*. According to Stuart's figures, and subject to the
deduction of the *c.*£18,000 reimbursed by Newcome for the palace
(which Stuart did not know about), Robinson in his lifetime and by
the terms of his will spent no more than *c.*£18,000 on the diocese of
Armagh.[131] This was of course a large sum; and of course Robinson
had not been under any obligation to spend anything. But it should
be weighed in the balance against the *c.*£75,000 (at least) in income
which Robinson drew between 1786 and 1794 from the diocese he
never saw. The accuracy of the net figure of *c.*£18,000 depends upon
the accuracy of the gross figure of £41,000 given by Stuart for
Robinson's benefactions to Armagh. This was certainly a complex cal-
culation, and it would be interesting to know how Stuart handled various problem items. He seems to be exercising due caution and
precision when writing of Robinson's benefaction to the new Armagh
Royal School building: where Chart baldly asserted that Robinson
'built and endowed a public school', Stuart stated more carefully that
Robinson 'advanced' £3,000 of the £5,000-plus which was required –
i.e. Robinson was *not* the sole benefactor and it looks as if his mone-
tary contribution was a loan, not a gift (apart, presumably, from the
gift of the site). The rural churches in the diocese to whose building
Robinson contributed financially are another grey area. Chart puts
the figure at four; Mohan puts it at eight.[132] There also seems to be
confusion between what Robinson obtained from the Board of First
Fruits and what he paid for out of his own pocket. For example,
Mohan states that Robinson 'built' Ballymakenny Church,
Co. Louth, but a Board minute of 5 June 1782 establishes that the
Board paid £500 to Robinson for Ballymakenny.[133] It is not clear how
Stuart treated this expenditure or calculated the number of churches.
Again, Henry Upton cites a case in which Robinson endowed a perpetual curacy *c.*1785 by forgoing a renewal fine of £2,000 for a lease
of the tithes of that parish.[134] Did Stuart know about this and did he
include this renunciation as part of Robinson's benefactions? There is
no way of knowing. However, it is reasonable to assume that, since
Stuart was very favourable to Robinson and was writing at a time
when there were still plenty of Robinson protégés about whom he
could consult and whose information would also be favourable,

Primate Robinson.

Reproduced from a mezzotint of 1835 by S.W. Reynolds
after the portrait of 1763 by Sir Joshua Reynolds
in the Synod Hall, Armagh.

Part of Canterbury quadrangle, Christ Church College, Oxford.
The three sides of the quadrangle, shown here,
were built at Robinson's expense between 1773 and 1783.

Photograph by Mrs Judith Curthoys.

Side-elevation of the Robinson, or Armagh Public, Library,
built by Robinson in 1771.

Photograph by Monuments and Buildings Record of Northern Ireland.

Bookplate of Primate Robinson, 1769, combining the arms of the see of Armagh (left) and the Robinson family's arms (right).

This armorial device is to be seen on many of Robinson's buildings.

John Hotham, bishop of Clogher, 1782–95 (but only a viceregal chaplain when he commented on Robinson's buildings in 1778).

Reproduced from an engraving after the original portrait of *c*.1790 by Gilbert Stuart.

A St Patrick's Cathedral
B The Parish Church
C Where St Peter and Paul Church stood
D Where St Columbus Church stood
E The New Meeting House
F The Old Meeting House
G The Market Cross
H The Market House
I The County gaol
K Where St Bridget's Church stood
L The Roman Chapple
M The Charter School
N The Old Abbey
O The Barracks
P The Vicar's Hall
Q Where the Temple Lafarta or
ye Church of Wonders stood
R Where St Bride's Church stood

John Rocque's *Plan of the City of Armagh*,
1760, reproduced by permission of the
Linen Hall Library.

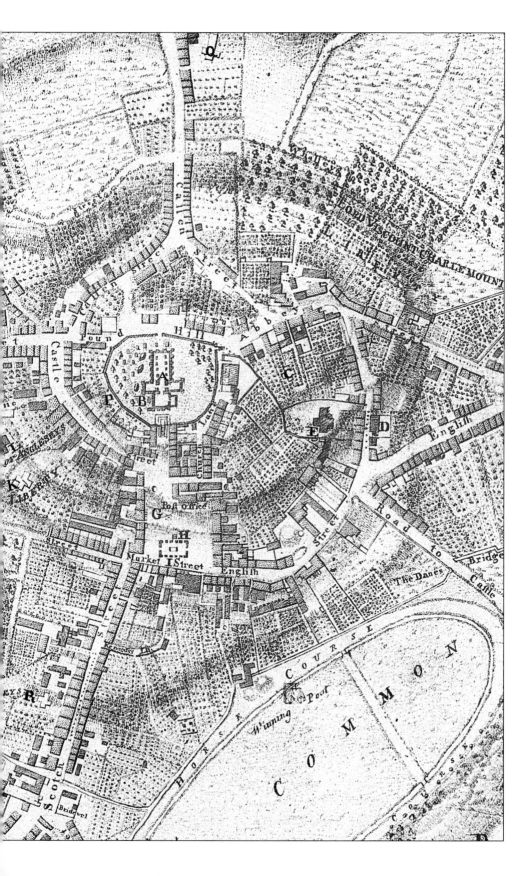

Garden front of The Palace, Armagh,
built by Robinson, 1766–70. The top storey was added in the 1820s.

Photograph by Monuments and Buildings Record of Northern Ireland.

The chapel built by Robinson near the west end of The Palace, 1781–6.

Photograph by Monuments and Buildings Record of Northern Ireland.

Primate Robinson.

Reproduced from a mezzotint of 1834 by S.W. Reynolds
after the portrait of 1775 by Sir Joshua Reynold.

Stuart is likely to have erred on the side of overstatement.

A special problem of interpretation attaches to the £5,000 which Robinson, famously, left for the establishment of a university in Armagh. During life, he had often maintained that 'The establishment of another University is the only permanent provision for the preservation of the Established Religion and indeed of the Protestant interest in Ireland', and that, without such a foundation, 'the teachers of the Established Religion will be the most illiterate teachers of the people in the kingdom'.[135] Yet, the £5,000 which he actually provided for its endowment was obviously inadequate to the purpose, and Robinson must have known that nothing would happen unless far more than matching finance were found elsewhere. A detailed scheme of endowment and incorporation was drawn up by Chief Secretary Pelham, c.1795–8. But it depended for its viability on a number of extremely doubtful expedients: the probably illegal raiding of the funds of the five royal schools in Ulster and of other educational charities; the appropriation of the incomes of one living in each of the dioceses in the metropolitan province of Armagh; and the distortion (again probably illegal) of Robinson's intentions by opening the university, its scholarships, fellowships and professorships, to dissenters. Not surprisingly, these various expedients raised as many enemies to the scheme as they did potential funds. These enemies included Newcome. Having been saddled with the cost of Robinson's palace, he cannot have been well disposed to any foundation which would have added lustre to Robinson's reputation. Nor can he have welcomed Pelham's proposed annexation of the incomes of livings in the province of Armagh, or his proposed raiding of the funds of Armagh and the other four royal schools (of one of which, Portora, in Enniskillen, Newcome's brother-in-law, the Rev. Dr Joseph Stock, was master until 1798). Significantly, when a more practical and less contentious scheme than Pelham's was submitted to Newcome in March 1799, he appears to have pigeon-holed it. The author of this alternative scheme was the Rev. Dr Thomas Carpendale, master of Armagh Royal School, 1786–1817. Carpendale made the interesting point that the whole of Ireland did not furnish sufficient scholars for the royal schools, and that the revenues of two of them could usefully be transferred to Robinson's university. He proposed that the

Armagh school buildings should provide its nucleus, and that he himself should be appointed its first provost at a salary of £500 per annum 'in addition to the £400 a year which I now receive as master out of the school lands'. On this basis, 'a respectable beginning' could be made if the government would add just £1,000 per annum to the interest on Robinson's £5,000.[136]

Under the terms of Robinson's will, the £5,000 was due to lapse in five years if the university had not been incorporated within that time. Carpendale's scheme was the only one which had a chance of meeting such a deadline, the more so as serious consideration does not seem to have been given to the problem until 1799. His scheme was flawed by blatant self-interest (although on his own showing Carpendale was academically qualified for the provostship); but this objection would not apply to Carpendale's successors as provost. However, Pelham's plan remained the only one on the tapis, and was still favoured by the Irish government after Pelham's departure from Ireland in 1797 and resignation as chief secretary in 1798. It also, and perhaps unexpectedly, received support from Robinson's Armagh-based executor, Archdeacon James A. Hamilton, who was the astronomer in Robinson's observatory from 1790 to 1815. Hamilton went along with the palpable distortion of Robinson's intentions by claiming that 'that truly wise and enlightened Prelate thought nothing would tend so much to conciliate and soften down the minds of our various sectaries in the North of Ireland, and bind them to the common interest of the Empire, as the foundation of a "Second University in the Province of Ulster"'.[137] The British government, however, took a different view, and rejected Pelham's scheme in late August 1799, when there was just a month to go.[138] In a long letter quashing the proposal, the Home Secretary, the 3rd Duke of Portland, included the quite fundamental objection (which he may have got from Agar): 'the legacy … is considered to be utterly inapplicable because … the Primate would [never] have contributed in any manner whatever to the establishment of an institution for the encouragement of Schismatics and Separatists from the Church'.[139] The £5,000 thus reverted to Robinson's family, and therefore has not been included in the figure of c.£18,000 at which Robinson's benefactions to the diocese of Armagh have been tentatively set. Stuart, whose purpose was to establish the extent of Robinson's generosity, almost certainly included the £5,000 in his total.

As a childless man, Robinson was in the same category as those other great benefactors of the Church in the eighteenth century, Archbishops King, Boulter and Bolton, John Stearne (bishop of Clogher, 1717–45) and Richard Pococke (bishop of Ossory, 1756–65).[140] While bishop of Derry (1691–1702), King bought for the diocese the library of his predecessor, Ezekiel Hopkins, and contributed to the cost of a building in which to accommodate it. While archbishop of Dublin, he founded and endowed a chair of divinity at TCD, and in the course of what Chart calls his 'parochial reformation' of the diocese of Dublin, sometimes purchased land for glebes himself and in general set 'a good example to the wealthy by generous contributions from his own purse'. In addition to these benefactions during his lifetime, he left all his property, to the value of nearly £17,000, to public charities when he died in 1729. According to Stuart, Boulter's 'charitable donations amounted, in the kingdom of Ireland alone, to above £40,000'. Bolton founded the Bolton Library, Cashel, restored the medieval cathedral on the Rock of Cashel, drained marshes in order to provide the city with a water supply, and had performed other good works in his two previous dioceses, all at his own expense. Stearne, among other acts of remarkable generosity, 'financed the completion of Clogher Cathedral …, provided capital to the … [Board of] First Fruits to purchase glebes and impropriations for resident incumbents …, [paid for] a printing-house and ten annual exhibitions [at TCD]' and left his books to Marsh's Library, Dublin. By his will, 'he disposed of about £50,000 in charity'. This computation almost certainly excluded the capital value of the Middletown estate, Co. Armagh, which he left as an endowment to the Stearne Charity, Middletown, and which had a rental of £1,226 per annum in 1820. Pococke, in addition to restoring St Canice's Cathedral in his lifetime, 'left his whole estate to the incorporated society at Lintown', Co. Kilkenny, an industrial school with an essentially proselytising agenda. If the comparison is extended into the nineteenth century, it must bring into the reckoning Primate Beresford, the most munificent childless prelate in Church of Ireland history, who is supposed to have given during the forty years of his primacy 'in excess of £280,000 to religious and charitable objects'.[141] As the inscription on the tomb of an English benefactor of an earlier age proclaimed, what was expected of such churchmen was not 'a widow's mite, but a bachelor's bounty'.[142]

Robinson differed fundamentally from these other childless benefactors in that he went out of his way to finance and endow two not-very-close relations and their respective dynasties of Robinson. He himself was the last survivor of the eight Robinson brothers, not one of whom had produced a son. The eldest brother, the mad Palladian, had eventually succeeded in alienating the family estate. His other great extravagance – besides Rokeby Park – was Ranelagh Gardens in London. Ranelagh, which was situated on the east side of Chelsea Hospital, 'was opened in 1742 under the auspices of Sir Thomas Robinson, ... dilettante statesman, architect, impresario and colonial governor, who was as remarkable for his dress as for his versatility, his favourite hunting costume, in which he appeared at Ranelagh and elsewhere, being a postilion's cap, a light green jacket and buckskin breeches'.[143] Having lost heavily in his Ranelagh speculation, he was placed under trusteeship by his brothers in the same year, 1742, and packed off to be governor of Barbados from then until 1747. But he committed fresh extravagances on his return, until it became necessary in 1769 to sell Rokeby Park and its accompanying estate.[144] Primate Robinson 'was much chagrined and displeased'. This was because that property would no longer be available for the support of the family baronetcy, which was destined to pass by special remainder at Robinson's death to his second cousin, Matthew (1713–1800). In spite of the alienation of Rokeby Park, Robinson chose 'Rokeby' as the title of the Irish barony conferred on him in 1777, and ensured that it, too, would pass by special remainder to Matthew. In his will, he left Matthew £10,000 to purchase a replacement estate in Yorkshire, and a total of £9,000-plus in legacies to other members and connections of the Robinson family in England. This was not really necessary. Matthew already had a Yorkshire estate called West Layton (near Rokeby Park), and a house and estate at Mount Norris, Kent; and a subsequent Lord Rokeby was due to succeed to the large estates, in Yorkshire and elsewhere, which Mrs Elizabeth Montagu (Matthew's sister) had been left by her husband in 1775.[145] So, there already were replacements for the loss of Rokeby Park.

In any case, none of the English Robinsons was Robinson's principal heir and residuary legatee. This was the Rev. John Freind (1754–1832), the son of Robinson's sister, Grace, and her husband, the Very Rev. Dr William Freind, an exceptionally undistinguished dean of Canterbury (1760–66).[146] Robinson had already provided well for this nephew out of the patronage of the primacy, making him prebendary of Tynan (diocese of Armagh) in 1778, archdeacon of Armagh in 1786, register of the prerogative court, etc. But he also left him the lease and contents of the Henrietta Street house, and settled on him (possibly in 1793, when Freind changed his name to Robinson) his long-leasehold estate in Co. Louth. Robinson had spent an estimated £30,000-plus in the mid-1780s on the purchase of this estate, and a definite £30,000 in the late 1780s and in 1793 respectively on the building of Rokeby Hall and a series of model farmhouses (the latter to the design of Francis Johnston).[147] From the mid-1780s on, Robinson's church-building and parochial endowing were also focused on the Louth estate. So it might be appropriate to regard these benefactions, too, as reflecting his role as a landowner and founder of an Irish family rather than as a diocesan. However, even if his outlay on the Louth estate be set at c.£60,000 only, this was still over three times his net benefactions to Armagh. Equally tellingly, the rental of the Louth estate stood at £2,264 per annum in 1839 – an income fully adequate to support the baronetcy conferred on the nephew in 1819. In short, Chart was quite mistaken in his view that Robinson, because he was a bachelor, devoted all his savings to his projects.

ROBINSON REASSESSED

FOR THE ABOVE AND OTHER REASONS, it is clear that Robinson's 'most distinguished and remarkable merits'[148] have been overrated. Flattery set in early – partly at Robinson's own instigation. Stuart, as well as Young, is a case in point. Stuart involves himself in the following euphemisms about Robinson: 'Lord Rokeby, has not, we believe, enriched the republic of letters by any important works of his own composition. The sermons which he sometimes preached were, both in style and in doctrine most excellent, but his voice was low and indistinctly heard.'[149] In plain English, he wrote nothing, and his occasional sermons were inaudible!

> Archbishop Simms calculated that his one surviving sermon would have taken fifty minutes to deliver. It must have been a painful experience for the House of Commons assembled in Christ Church Cathedral in 1757. His English style is far from lucid and his sentence construction convoluted, especially when he attempted philosophy. As Archbishop Simms noted, he never once used the name of Jesus Christ throughout the sermon, and its theological content is minimal ... He loved books about him ... [but] one does not detect great reflective powers or much depth in scholarship. Indeed, Dr Johnson said of him that he was 'not esteemed a man of much professional learning or a liberal patron of it' ... His mind seems to have been more practical than theoretical.[150]

Robinson was 'a colossal man', tall and stately, with a magnificent bearing and 'a penetrating eye'.[151] He knew how to deploy these attributes to the best effect, and it may well be that people like Lords

Hillsborough and Buckinghamshire, who praised his judgement, *gravitas* and statesmanship, mistook appearance for reality. The mistake was easily made, because – as has recently been argued – Robinson seems to have deliberately cultivated his image. He was painted three times by Reynolds (setting aside a number of variants of the second and third portraits). The first, painted in 1758, when Robinson was still in his first bishopric, Killala, shows a cold, proud, inscrutable and calculating man. Not until the second (1763) and, particularly, the third (1775) is the expression softened by benignity, real or affected. The second shows the benign scholar among his books – the image of Robinson for which Archbishop Simms fell;[152] the third shows the benign improver in his landscape.[153] But was Robinson benign at all? Richard Cumberland, who struggled to think the best of his host when on a visit to Armagh *c*.1772–4 recorded, in a famous and damning passage: 'After Divine service, the officiating clergy presented themselves in the hall of his Palace to pay their court. I asked him how many were to dine with us. He answered, "Not one"; he did them kindness[es], but he gave them no entertainments; they were in excellent discipline.'[154] Horace Walpole called him 'proud and superficial', and a modern commentator 'distant ... somewhat proud and a little dull'.[155] The distantness and formality may also have masked insecurity: Robinson ordered all his personal papers and correspondence to be destroyed – an action which surely betrays a want of confidence in his own views and actions. The distantness and formality certainly denoted a lack of any sense of humour. There does not appear to be any recorded instance of Robinson's cracking a joke. In June 1787, when contradicting a rumour that he was dying at Bath, Mrs Agar said that he was reputedly 'alive and *merry*', and the fact that she underlined 'merry' speaks for itself. It may be that Robinson had been a merrier man in younger days, but that the ridicule and embarrassment created by the antics of his eldest brother, Sir Thomas, had contributed – along with Robinson's promotion – to his withdrawal into stuffiness and formality.

Robinson, plainly, did not deserve Primate Simms's often-quoted tribute that, as primate, he 'was a public rather than a political figure', or Mant's conclusion that he did not take 'a prominent part in the political administration of affairs'. It is true that, because of changed political circumstances, he was not formally involved in the government of the country, as his predecessors had been; nor did he personally follow the bad example of his immediate predecessor, Stone, by setting himself up as a party leader. It was not in him to be a party leader. He was probably bad at thinking on his feet; and, where Stone had shown the most amazing resilience, Robinson disliked opposition, confrontation and getting hard knocks. When confronted, he tended to back off, as he did with Bedford in 1761, with Hely-Hutchinson (after Robinson's ally and activist, Attorney-General Tisdall, died in 1777), and with Agar (once Robinson had failed to block Agar's promotion to an archbishopric in 1779). He did, however, resemble Stone in his 'Machiavellian cunning and hypocrisy'; and many examples of his practising of these arts have been given.

He was also far from being above the lowest political manoeuvres – as witness his passion for exploiting bishops' boroughs. The cases of Old Leighlin in 1761 and Armagh in 1768 have been cited, but his weakness for parliamentary patronage did not end with them. In 1782, when his Co. Armagh friend and neighbour, the Rev. Dr Walter Cope of Drumilly, near Loughgall, was appointed bishop of Ferns, it was suggested that 'the Primate got Cope to Ferns' and that 'most probably they have taken care of the two [Old Leighlin] seats for next general election'.[156] Cope did indeed flout the wishes of the government over the return for Old Leighlin, notably at a by-election in 1787.[157] In Armagh borough itself at the general election of 1783, Robinson suited himself rather than the government of the day in his choice of MPs. One of them, Colonel George Rawson, later 'gave several votes against' the Castle on the Regency in February–March 1789; the other, Henry Meredyth, either absented himself deliberately or, more probably, was too old and ill to attend (either way, he was no help to the government).[158] Robinson was at this time understandably incensed at Buckingham's assault on the Church. But he wrote most disingenuously from Bath in mid-March 1789, in response to Buckingham's request that he assist with his proxy to defeat the

> strong party ... formed in opposition to the administration of the King's government in Ireland ... My disposition to resist such a mischievous combination by every means in my power cannot be

doubted. I will not therefore attempt to describe the great anxiety of my mind, when I acquaint you that I cannot give the assistance that is desired by proxy, consistently with my constant practice on former applications. I must rely on your Excellency's favourable construction of the reasons that have induced me frequently to avow my decided indisposition to sign a proxy on any occasion.

Buckingham by no means put a 'favourable construction' on this refusal, particularly in view of the record of Robinson's two MPs, and shortly afterwards urged in vain that Robinson should be excluded from the 'compliment' of being appointed one of the lords justices. In all these instances, Robinson did not behave like 'a public rather than a political figure', far less like a venerable elder statesman.

He was 'publicly ambitious of great deeds' and, as Hotham noted, insatiable in his desire for praise on that account. To a man of Robinson's temperament, building was a softer path to celebrity than politics, and Armagh City, where he encountered none but admirers and yes-men, was the ideal theatre for his building operations. Yet, even in Armagh, he was not the great builder and benefactor he has been cracked up to be. His importance as a builder lies in the force of his example, his planning and encouragement and the covenants in his building leases, not so much in the amount of his own money which he spent. Nor does he stand comparison (particularly in relation to their respective resources) with the other childless benefactors in Church of Ireland history. His biggest beneficiary was his own family, not the Church or charities.

As a Church leader he was unexceptional. He achieved much as a 'graceful' administrative reformer in the first twelve years of his primacy; and as an adviser from the sidelines in the critical year of 1788, when he was almost eighty, he showed tactical and political skill. But his feebleness and evasiveness as a political leader are indefensible. They are also hard to explain. Retaining the favour of the government for a variety of self-interested reasons – including the advancement of his nephew – may have been one motive from the mid-1770s onwards. From then on, Robinson may also have welcomed opportunities of wrong-footing Agar, particularly if he really thought his own illnesses of the late 1780s serious enough to make a vacancy in the primacy imminent. However, his reluctance to act or speak out on the subject of the Catholic Relief Act of 1792 is not explicable on grounds of 'jealousy and perhaps envy' of Agar, since many besides Agar were opposed to it, and since it was not a measure for which the King had any enthusiasm. Moreover, the alarmist fears of Irish catholic conspiracy which had been the theme of Robinson's 'croaking' in the mid-1780s had hardly diminished with the passage of time and the approach of a new world war. A man who, after thirty-seven years' membership of the House of Lords, could say that he had never given his proxy must have been reluctant to take a decisive part. Something of this is also evident in his aloofness from the turbulent and increasingly sectarian politics of Co. Armagh from the late 1770s onwards. All in all, it is hard to account for Robinson's abnegation of his political leadership of the Church except on the basis of a psychological reluctance to stand up and be counted.

In September 1793, it was claimed that 'the Primate's age and infirmities' precluded him from attending to serious Church business. He was eighty-four in 1793, and for some years past had been behaving like a man who was old, tired and anxious to be allowed to enjoy his 'emoluments' and his ill-health in peace. Age, however, is a factor which needs to be borne in mind throughout his time at Armagh. He was fifty-six when he attained the primacy. Reynolds's second portrait of him, painted in 1763, when he was still bishop of Kildare, shows a seated man who would nowadays be called old. Reynolds's third portrait of him, painted in 1775 (when 'age', according to Walpole, had 'softened [him] into a beauty'), actually makes him look younger, because he is standing up and something of his imposing physical stature comes out from the canvas. Robinson may have been old, or at any rate valetudinarian, before his time. In any case, no man who had learnt the trade of Irish politics in the early 1750s could possibly have felt at home in a world dominated by the catholic question and in which the British government espoused the catholic cause. Nor could any primate have felt at home in a Church dominated by a much junior archbishop, whose promotion he had notoriously endeavoured to prevent. It is likely that his permanent retreat from Ireland was a reaction, conscious or subconscious, to the ascendancy of Agar. More generally, Robinson in his last decade was one of a number of senior churchmen of that era who were victims as well as beneficiaries of a system which assumed that incumbents would die in harness, and which had made no provision – as the Roman Catholic Church in Ireland had done since at least the seventeenth century – for coadjutorships (in the precise meaning of that term, not the loose sense in which Robinson used it).[159] As 'a very tough incumbent in fine preservation', Robinson long outlived the usefulness he had exhibited during the first twelve or so years of his primacy.

Why, then, has his reputation remained high and has he become the best-known and even the most admired of the Church of Ireland primates? Much of the explanation lies in simple misunderstanding of the facts and watersheds of his career: it has not been appreciated that he went quiet from 1779 and missing from 1786. Nor has it been appreciated that the vast majority of his archiepiscopal wealth was spent on his family and himself, not on his archiepiscopal projects. In Armagh city his expenditure (such as it was in relative terms), and especially his influence and example, undoubtedly made a major difference; and there he is always likely to be a cult figure because of the importance of the building ventures associated with him to a city currently as dependent for its prosperity on tourism as it once was on linen and archiepiscopal patronage. But this indulgence is unlikely to be extended to his historical reputation in the broader contexts of Church, political and even architectural history. When his jealous refusal to make what would now be called 'succession-planning' for the Church of Ireland, and his abandonment of its headship during his latter years, are weighed in the balance with his buildings, and when his buildings are measured against both the highest standards and the vast extent of his resources, there is little doubt that he will be found wanting.

NOTES

1. This paragraph is mainly based on A.P.W. Malcomson, *Archbishop Charles Agar: Churchmanship and Politics in Ireland, 1760–1810* (Dublin, 2002), pp. 134–5 and 138.

2. Horace Walpole to Sir Horace Mann, 20 Dec. 1764, printed in Peter Cunningham (ed.), *The Letters of Horace Walpole* (9 vols, London, 1857–9), IV, p. 303.

3. Hillsborough to Henry Fox, [early June 1762], printed in Earl of Ilchester (ed.), *Letters to Henry Fox, [1st] Lord Holland ...* (Roxburghe Club, London, 1915), pp. 152–3.

4. This paragraph is mainly based on Malcomson, *op. cit.*, pp. 139–40.

5. Quoted in Rev. Christopher Mohan, 'Archbishop Richard Robinson: Builder of Armagh', in *Seanchas Ard Mhacha*, VI, no. 1 (1971), p. 96.

6. John Scott to Welbore Ellis, 4 Dec. 1778, Normanton papers, PRONI, T/3719/C/12/29.

7. Stone to Bedford, 27 Mar. 1759, printed in *Eighteenth Century Irish Official Papers in Great Britain. Private Collections, Volume Two* (HMSO, Belfast, 1990), p. 218.

8. Robinson to Bedford, 28 Mar. 1761, *ibid.*, p. 264.

9. Bedford to Robinson, 4 Apr. 1761, *ibid.*, p. 265.

10. Robert E. Burns, *Irish Parliamentary Politics in the Eighteenth Century [1714–60]* (2 vols, Washington DC, 1989–90), II, pp. 298–314.

11. Rigby to Bedford, 30 Mar. 1761, *Irish Official Papers*, II, pp. 264–5.

12. Jackson to Bedford, 2 Apr. 1761, *ibid.*, p. 265.

13. Autobiography of Thomas Newton, Bishop of Bristol, printed in Adam Clarke (ed.), *[Compendium Edition of] the Lives of ... Newton ... [etc.], and of the Rev. Philip Skelton by Mr [Samuel] Burdy* (2 vols, London, 1816), vol. II, p. 157.

14. Rigby to Sir Robert Wilmot, 13 and 16 Apr. 1761, Wilmot papers, PRONI, T/3019/4358 and 4361.

15. Mrs Montagu to her husband, Edward, 20 Dec. 1764, printed in Reginald Blunt (ed.), *Mrs Montagu, 'Queen of the Blues': her Letters and Friendships from 1762 to 1800* (2 vols, London, 1923), I, pp. 120–21. For a similar indictment, see Rev. James Gordon, *A History of Ireland from the earliest Times to ... 1801* (2 vols, London, 1806), II, p. 222.

16. Mohan, *op. cit.*, p. 127. Father Mohan's source for this pattern of meetings relates to 1783, but Mrs Montagu states that Robinson had been doing it 'always'.

17. Walpole to Mann, 20 Dec. 1764, *op. cit.*, pp. 303–4; *The Georgian Society*

Records of Eighteenth-Century Domestic Architecture and Decoration in Dublin, II (reprint, Dublin, 1969), p. 12. The eyewitness was his friend, George Montagu, when on a visit to Ireland in 1761–3. Since the house had been built for Primate Boulter and was occupied by the next three primates – Hoadly, Stone and Robinson – Henrietta Street in their day was sometimes called 'Primate's Hill'. See *Georgian Society Records*, II, pp. 12–13 and 63–4.

18   Mohan, *op. cit.*, p. 99.

19   Quoted in *ibid.*, p. 98.

20   William Gerard Hamilton (Northumberland's chief secretary) to John Hely-Hutchinson, 2 Dec. 1764 [misprinted as 1769], *HMC, Eighth Report, Appendix, Part II* [Emly (Pery) papers] (1881), p. 191.

21   Grenville 'irritated George III more than any other prime minister he ever had' – Richard Pares, *King George* III *and the Politicians* (Oxford, 1953), p. 145. See also pp. 147n. and 152n., and P.J. Jupp, *Lord Grenville (1759–1834)* (Oxford, 1985), pp. 7–8.

22   Walpole to Mann, 20 Dec. 1764, *op. cit.*, pp. 303–4.

23   Quoted in G.O. Simms, Archbishop of Armagh, 'The Founder of Armagh's Public Library: Primate Robinson among his Books', in *Irish Booklore*, I, no. I (1971), pp. 142 and 145.

24   Quoted in *ibid.*, p. 142.

25   Walpole to Mann, 13 Jan. 1765, *op. cit.*, pp. 310–11.

26   William James Smith (ed.), *The Grenville Papers: being the Correspondence of Richard Grenville, Earl Temple, K.G., and the Rt Hon. George Grenville, their Friends and Contemporaries* (4 vols, London, 1852), II, pp. 533–5. I am indebted for this reference to Mr Peter MacDonagh.

27   Clarke, *op. cit.*, II, p. 156.

28   George (later Sir George and Lord) Macartney to Fox, 14 Oct. 1763, *Letters to Henry Fox*, p. 187.

29   Edmond Sexten Pery to Robert FitzGerald, 31 Jan. 1765, printed in M.A. Hickson (ed.), *Old Kerry Records ... second Series* (2 vols, London, 1874), II, p. 279.

30   Peter MacDonagh, '"Hostile, indigested innovations": official pressures for reform of the Church of Ireland in the 1780s' (forthcoming article). I am most grateful to Mr MacDonagh for his generosity in sending me this important paper in draft. There are only a couple of points (such as this interpretation of Robinson's appointment) about which I have any reservations.

31   Hardwicke to the prime minister, Newcastle, 29 Dec. 1754, Newcastle papers, British Library, Add. Ms. 32737, ff. 516–17.

32   D.H. Akenson, *The Church of Ireland: Ecclesiastical Reform and Revolution, 1800–85* (Yale, 1971), pp. 74–145.

33   E.M. Johnston[-Liik] (ed.), 'The state of the Irish parliament, 1784–7', in *Proceedings of the Royal Irish Academy*, vol. 71, sec. C, no. 5 (Dublin, 1971), p. 166.

34   Thomas Waite to Wilmot, [*c*.1766?], Wilmot papers, PRONI, T/3019/6069.

35   It would be a very big coincidence if the Princess Dowager's collection was not the source of the dozen or so portraits of Stuart and Hanoverian royalty which were given to Robinson to hang in the new palace he built in Armagh in 1768–70. Plaques on the magnificently framed studio copies of Allan Ramsay's coronation portraits of George III and Queen Charlotte, which hang in the hall of the palace (now the headquarters of Armagh City Council) to this day, declare that they were presented to Robinson by the King and Queen in 1772 (the year of the Princess Dowager's death). The Royal Archives, Windsor, holds no inventory of the Princess Dowager's effects at the time of her death, or earlier. But it may be no coincidence that the half-length portrait of her husband, Frederick, Prince of Wales (d. 1751), is one of the best in the Armagh collection (as is the similarly sized portrait of Prince George of Denmark): the studio copies of the Ramsay full-lengths are good, but no better than all the others dispatched to British embassies in Europe and British government houses throughout the empire; and most of the copies of seventeenth-century royalty are bad and painted at many removes from the original. For a tour of the portraits and the palace, I am grateful to Mr Isaac Beattie of the Palace Stables Heritage Centre, Armagh, and for help with the problems of provenance to Miss Pamela Clark, Registrar, the Royal Archives, Windsor.

36   John William Stubbs, *The History of the University of Dublin from its Foundation to the End of the Eighteenth Century ...* (Dublin, 1889), pp. 227–9 and 239–40.

37   Lords justices, excluding Robinson, were appointed on 22 Feb. 1765, but this was before his enthronement.

38   Robinson to the Lord Lieutenant, the 2nd Earl of Buckinghamshire, 11 June 1777, Heron papers, NLI, Ms. 13035/7.

39   Quoted in MacDonagh, *op. cit.*, p. 4.

40   Hillsborough to Buckinghamshire, 20 Jan. 1777, *HMC Lothian Mss.*, p. 298. Hillsborough's letter, possibly written at Robinson's prompting, urged Buckinghamshire to appoint Robinson to the linen board.

41   Buckinghamshire to Sir Charles Hotham Thompson, 11 Mar. 1777, Hotham papers, PRONI, T/3429/1/8.

42   John Garnett, bishop of Clogher, to Townshend, 6 Feb. 1772, Townshend letter-book, RCB Library, Ms. 20/9; Agar to Robinson, 15 Jan. 1788, T/3719/C/22/1; 1st Marquess of Buckingham (the Lord Lieutenant) to Archbishop Fowler, 10 Apr. 1788, Stowe papers, Huntington Library, San Marino, California, STG, box 29; Akenson, *Church of Ireland*, p. 59.

43   Hon. Thomas Fitzmaurice to [Rev. Samuel] Riall, 19 July 1776, Riall papers, NLI, Ms. 8395.

44   Hon. and Rev. Archdeacon James St Leger to Agar, 20 Sep. 1808, T/3719/C/42/69; Isaac Mann, bishop of Cork, to 2nd Earl of Shannon, 31 Jan. 1786, Shannon papers, PRONI, D/2707/A2/2/100.

45   Rev. Euseby Cleaver to Charles O'Hara, 3 Oct. [1786], O'Hara papers, PRONI, T/2812/18/21.

46   Clarke, *op. cit.*, II, 429. I am grateful to the Rev. Dr W.G. Neely for drawing this passage to my attention.

47   Mohan, *Archbishop Richard Robinson*, p. 120; W.A. Phillips (ed.), *A History of the Church of Ireland* (3 vols, Oxford, 1933–4), III, p. 245. The chapter in which Robinson features is by D.A. Chart.

48   Robinson to Orde, 19 Jan. 1785, Bolton papers, NLI, Ms. 17350, ff. 71–2.

49   Mohan, *op. cit.*, pp. 121–2 and 124.

50   Quoted in R.B. McDowell, *Ireland in the Age of Imperialism and Revolution, 1760–1801* (Oxford, 1979), p. 161.

51   Clarke, *op. cit.*, II, p. 155.

52   *List of the Absentees ...* (Dublin, 1767), p. 9. This pamphlet was further updated in a new edition, where Robinson again features, published in Dublin in 1769. The quotation is from T.C. Barnard, *A New Anatomy of Ireland: the Irish Protestants, 1649–1770* (Yale, 2003), p. 100.

53   'Titles of the several acts of parliament passed at the instance of the late Primate Robinson', [1794?], Armagh Diocesan Registry papers, PRONI, DIO 4/11/5/1; 'A list [made in 1800] of the acts of parliament for ecclesiastical purposes prepared by Dr Charles Agar, Archbishop of Cashel', in Agar's 'state' of the diocese of Cashel, 1779–1801, 21 M 57/B6/1. The list of Robinson's acts given by Mohan (p. 124) is seriously and misleadingly incomplete.

54   'Scheme of indemnification given to Mr Orde' (the Chief Secretary), 19 Feb. 1787, 21 M 57/B31/21; Thomas Orde to Agar, 14 Feb. 1787, T/3719/C/21/10; and Welbore Ellis to Agar, 10 Mar. 1787, T/3719/C/21/12.

55   E.M. Johnston-Liik, *History of the Irish Parliament, 1692–1800: Commons, Constituencies and Statutes* (6 vols, Belfast, 2002), V, pp. 245–6.

56   I am grateful to Dr T.C. Barnard for informing me that Sir Christopher Wren and Sir John Vanbrugh had both condemned intramural burials in London churches as long ago as 1711.

57   Scott to Welbore Ellis, 4 Dec. 1778, T/3719/C/12/29.

58   Malcomson, *op. cit.*, *passim*.

59   John Hamilton to Agar, 8 Dec. 1778, T/3719/C/12/43.

60   Scott to Ellis, 4 Dec. 1778, T/3719/C/12/29.

61 Shannon to James Dennis, 28 Feb. 1779, Shannon papers, PRONI, D/2707/A/2/3/56.

62 Agar to Robinson, 6 June 1771, T/3719/C/5/1.

63 Notes containing the substance of Agar's speech, 22 May 1772, 21 M 57/A5/5.

64 I am indebted for this information to Dr James Kelly.

65 Quoted in Mohan, *op. cit.*, p. 125.

66 21 M 57/A5/3/1.

67 Ellis to Agar, 18 Mar. 1774; Robert Waller to Sir George Macartney, 19 Mar. 1774, printed in Thomas Bartlett (ed.), *Macartney in Ireland, 1768–72: a Calendar of the Chief Secretaryship Papers of Sir George Macartney* (Belfast, 1978), pp. 187–8.

68 Buckinghamshire to Lord George Germain, 5 May 1778, NLI, Ms. 13036/8.

69 For a detailed discussion of these issues, see Malcomson, *op. cit.*, pp. 223–9.

70 Unless otherwise stated, this section is based on *ibid.*, pp. 148–58.

71 Hely-Hutchinson to Agar, 24 Nov. 1778, T/3719/C/12/21; Stubbs, *op. cit.*, pp. 239–40.

72 Heron to Buckinghamshire, 29 Mar. 1779, NLI, Heron papers, Ms. 13037/6.

73 O'Beirne to Agar, 9 Nov. 1801, T/3719/C/35/28.

74 The 10th Earl of Westmorland (a subsequent lord lieutenant) to William Pitt, the Prime Minister, [pre-5 Sep. 1794], PRO 30/8/331, ff. 310–15.

75 Robinson to Agar, 14 Aug. 1779, T/3719/C/13/34.

76 *Ibid.*, 8 July 1780, T/3719/C/14/23.

77 Rev. Peter Galloway, *The Most Illustrious Order of St Patrick, 1783–1983* (Chichester, 1983), p. 13. I am grateful to Dr Neely for drawing this passage to my attention.

78 Robinson to Agar, 23 May 1788, T/3719/C/22/19.

79 Agar to Macartney, 1 Feb. 1780, *Macartney in Ireland*, p. 327. The Archbishop proposed this, or some such amendment, in the British Privy Council, but was outvoted – Heron to Buckinghamshire, 10 Mar. 1780, Ms. 13039/4.

80 *Journals of the House of Lords of the Kingdom of Ireland* (8 vols, Dublin, 1780–1800), V, p. 171.

81 Robinson to Agar, 8 July 1780, T/3719/C/14/23.

82 Agar's draft for, and a printed version of, the Lords' protest, 19 Aug. 1780, 21 M 57/A14/15–16; *ibid.*, 3 May 1782, 21 M 57/A14/1 and B28/2; *Lords' Journals*, V, pp. 216–17 and 320–21.

83   Gerard O'Brien (ed.), *Catholic Ireland in the Eighteenth Century: Collected Essays of Maureen Wall* (Dublin, 1989), pp. 140 and 144; F.G. James, *Lords of the Ascendancy: the Irish House of Lords and its Members, 1600–1800* (Dublin, 1995), pp. 139–40.

84   Mohan, *op. cit.*, pp. 97–8, quoting a letter of 26 January from the Countess of Moira.

85   Quoted by Dr Neely in 'Richard Robinson', a talk given to the Armagh Clerical Society in 1994. I am very grateful to Dr Neely for sending me a copy of the text of this talk.

86   Scott, now Lord Earlsfort, to Agar, 1 Nov. 1784, T/3719/C/18/40; Malcomson, *John Foster: the Politics of the Anglo-Irish Ascendancy* (Oxford, 1978), p. 440 (citing and commenting on a highly alarmist letter from Robinson to Chief Secretary Orde, 19 Jan. 1785, NLI, Bolton papers, Ms. 16350, ff. 71–2).

87   Rutland to Sydney, 7 Oct. 1784, *HMC Rutland Mss.*, III, 141.

88   Unless otherwise stated, this section is based on Malcomson, *Archbishop Charles Agar*, pp. 230–40 and 248–54.

89   Ellis to Agar, 22 Sep. 1786, T/3719/C/20/29.

90   Robinson to Agar, 27 Jan. 1787, T/3719/C/21/9.

91   Scott to Agar, 19 May 1783, T/3719/C/17/15.

92   Phillips, *op. cit.*, III, p. 244.

93   The whole of this paragraph is taken from A.G. McCartney's admirable recent study, *The Organs and Organists of the Cathedral Church of St Patrick, Armagh, 1482–1998* (Armagh, 1999), pp. 5–16.

94   Neely, *op. cit.*

95   James Stuart, author of *Historical Memoirs of the City of Armagh for a Period of 1373 Years …* (Newry, 1819).

96   Mohan, *op. cit.*, pp. 107–8, quoting from Stuart, *op. cit.*, pp. 449–50, and from an unspecified issue of *The Newry Magazine*.

97   Phillips, *op. cit.*, III, pp. 244–5 and 277.

98   C.E.B. Brett, *Buildings of Co. Armagh* (Belfast, 1999), p. 47 and, for the cathedral in general, pp. 47–50.

99   Mohan, *loc. cit.*

100   Phillips, *loc. cit.*

101   *Journals of the Rev. John Wesley …* (London, 1836), p. 736. I am indebted to Ms Catherine McCullough, Curator of Armagh County Museum, for drawing this latter source to my attention.

102   Neely, *op. cit.*

103   McParland, *Public Architecture in Ireland, 1680–1760* (Yale, 2001), p. 41.

104   Hotham to Hotham Thompson, 19 Oct. 1778, Hotham papers, PRONI, T/3429/2/3.

105   Rev. Dr Richard Norris to Robinson, 27 May 1794, PRONI, DIO 4/8/9/3/24.

106   Buckingham to Archbishop Fowler, 10 Apr. 1788, Stowe papers, STG, box 29.

107   Stuart, *op. cit.*, p. 453.

108   Young, *A Tour in Ireland* ... (London, 1780), subscription list and pp. 103–4 – the subscription list is highly significant, and is a unique feature of this London first edition; *Journals of the Rev. John Wesley*, p. 736.

109   James Kelly (ed.), *The Letters of Lord Chief Baron Edward Willes to the Earl of Warwick, 1757–62* ... (Aberystwyth, 1990), pp. 31–2.

110   This is a crude and partial summary of the results of comparisons being made by Mr Sean Barden of Armagh County Museum between and among: John Rocque's printed *Plan of the City of Armagh*, 1760; a copy of a 'Map of the City of Armagh surveyed by order of ... the Lord Primate ... 1766 by Robert Livingston ...' (Armagh County Museum); and 'A List of the Inhabitants of the Town of Armagh for the use of ... the Lord Primate, 1770' by Rev. William Lodge (Armagh Public Library). I am most grateful to Mr Barden for making his results-to-date available to me.

111   Robert McKinstry *et al.*, *The Buildings of Armagh* (UAHS, Belfast, 1992), *passim*; Stuart, *op. cit.*, pp. 443–4.

112   I am indebted for this point to Professor B.M.S. Campbell.

113   For the completely different situation in the borough and city of Cashel, see Malcomson, *Archbishop Charles Agar*, pp. 286–95 and 333.

114   Stuart to William Elliot (the Chief Secretary), 8 Apr. 1806, *HMC Dropmore Mss.*, VIII, pp. 90–93.

115   *John Wesley's Journals*, p. 736.

116   Hotham to Hotham Thompson, 17 Aug. and 19 Oct. 1778, PRONI, T/3429/2/2–3.

117   George Otto Simms, archbishop of Armagh, 'Archbishop Robinson': text of a lecture given in the Synod Hall, Church House, Armagh, on 22 June 1971. I am indebted to Dr Neely for a copy of this text.

118   Copies of a memorial from Robinson to the Lords Justices, 4 Aug. 1766, of a warrant from them to Robinson, 12 Aug. 1766, and of a certificate from the Lord Lieutenant to Robinson, 23 Dec. 1775, DIO 4/40/5/1, 2 and 8.

119   [John Campbell], *A Philosophical Survey of the South of Ireland in a Series of Letters to John Watkinson, M.D.* (Dublin, 1778), p. 132. By contrast, the Rev. Dr D.A. Beaufort, a better judge because he was an amateur architect, commented in 1787 that the palace 'appears very ill-designed for the expense ... There are but six bedrooms; his Grace's is below. The drawing-room [is] too small, the hall neither hall nor parlour. Out of the house, the

grounds have a fine outline [and] are prettily planted ... But the garden is horribly placed in front of the house ... [He] has lately built very near it a neat and pretty chapel with a handsome portico of the ancient Ionic order' – Beaufort's tour journal, Sep.–Dec. 1787, TCD Library: microfilm copy in PRONI, MIC/250, pp. 73–4. For the architectural merits of the palace and chapel, see Brett, *Buildings of Co. Armagh*, pp. 32–3 and 122–3, and the UAHS *Buildings of Armagh*, pp. 171–6.

120   Joseph R. Fisher and John H. Robb, *Royal Belfast Academical Institution: Centenary Volume, 1810–1910* (Belfast, 1913), p. 24. Fisher is here quoting or paraphrasing Reid's *History of the Presbyterian Church*, but neither Reid nor he realised that the £15,000–£16,000 was connected with the palace. I am grateful to Sir Peter Froggatt for drawing my attention to this source.

121   *Ibid.*

122   Stuart, then bishop of St David's, to the King, 16 July 1800, *Later Correspondence of George* III, III, p. 377.

123   The warrant of 12 Aug. 1766 from the Lords Justices to Robinson (DIO 4/40/5/2) specifically authorises the change of primatial residence from Drogheda to Armagh.

124   Richard Cumberland, *Memoirs* (London, 1806), p. 172.

125   Simms, 'Archbishop Robinson'.

126   *Georgian Society Records*, III, p. 87 mentions that the previous tenant, Lord Chancellor Lifford, quitted Belvedere in 1769.

127   *Georgian Society Records*, II, p. 13. I am grateful to Dr James Kelly for showing me Belvedere, which now constitutes the nucleus of St Patrick's College, Drumcondra.

128   M. Craig, *Classic Irish Houses of the Middle Size* (London, 1976), p. 152.

129   Simms, *Primate Robinson*, pp. 144–5; H.L. Thompson, *Christ Church* (Oxford, 1900), pp. 165–6; Antony Dale, *James Wyatt, Architect, 1746–1813* (Oxford, 1936), pp. 33–4. I am grateful to Mrs Judith Curthoys, Archivist, Christ Church, for showing me 'Canterbury' quadrangle (Robinson was actually responsible for only three sides of it) and the Christ Church bust of Robinson in February 2003.

130   Peter Roebuck, *Yorkshire Baronets, 1640–1760: Families, Estates and Fortunes* (Oxford, 1980), pp. 28, 50, 58, 269–70 and 310; Christopher Hussey, *English Country Houses ..., 1715–60* (London, 1955), pp. 123–6; Nikolaus Pevsner, *The Buildings of England: Yorkshire – the North Riding* (reprint, Harmondsworth, 1973), pp. 309–10; Emily J. Climenson (ed.), *Elizabeth Montagu ...: her Correspondence from 1720 to 1761* (2 vols, London, 1906), II, pp. 275–7.

131   Stuart, *Armagh*, pp. 444–57.

132   Phillips, *op. cit.*, III, 245; Mohan, *op. cit.*, pp. 108–9.

133   Mohan, *op. cit.*, p. 109; PRONI, DIO 4/11/12/53.

134   DIO 4/11/5/1.

135   Robinson to Agar, 29 Apr. 1787, T/3719/C/21/17. For the background to this declaration, see James Kelly, 'The context and course of Thomas Orde's Plan of Education of 1787', in *The Irish Journal of Education*, XX, no. 1 (1986), p. 19.

136   Carpendale to [Newcome], 26 Mar. and 10 Apr. 1799, Primate Stuart papers, Bedfordshire and Luton RO, WY 994/2–4.

137   Hamilton to Cornwallis, 24 Aug. 1798, printed in 3rd Marquess of Londonderry (ed.), *Memoirs and Correspondence of Viscount Castlereagh …* (first ser., 4 vols, London, 1848–9), I, pp. 319–20. Hamilton was himself a victim of inadequate endowment: although Robinson provided adequately for the observatory, the astronomer depended for his livelihood on preferment in the diocese and anything else he could obtain (in Hamilton's case, the prebend of Mullabrack and the archdeaconry of Ross – Canon James B. Leslie, *Armagh Clergy and Parishes …* [Dundalk, 1911], pp. 62 and 446–7).

138   Fisher and Robb, *op. cit.*, pp. 24–9.

139   Portland to Cornwallis, 31 Aug. 1799, *Castlereagh Correspondence*, II, pp. 381–6.

140   This and the next paragraph are based almost entirely on Malcomson, *Archbishop Charles Agar*, pp. 456–8.

141   Canon W.E.C. Fleming, *Armagh Clergy, 1800–2000 …* (Dundalk, 2001), p. 37.

142   Quoted in J. Meadows Cowper, *The Lives of the Deans of Canterbury, 1541 to 1900 …* (Canterbury, 1900), p. 63. The benefactor concerned was Thomas Neville, dean of Canterbury, 1597–1615.

143   Hon. Evan Charteris, *William Augustus, Duke of Cumberland, His Early Life and Times* (London, 1913), p. 96.

144   Ironically, Rokeby Park is best known because of its association with families other than the Robinsons. Sir Thomas sold it to John Sawrey Morritt (d. 1791), whose son and successor, John Bacon Sawrey Morritt, was a friend of Walter Scott and the inspiration and dedicatee of the latter's historical poem, *Rokeby*. According to Scott, 'This ancient manor long [ago] gave [their] name to a family by whom it is said to have been possessed from the Conquest downward and who are at different times distinguished in history … The Rokeby, or Rokesby, family … [remained there] until the great civil war when, having embraced the cause of Charles I, they suffered severely by fines and confiscations. The estate then passed from its ancient possessors to the family of the Robinsons, from whom it was purchased by the father of my valued friend, the present proprietor … The scene … [of] this poem … is laid in his beautiful demesne … The ancient castle of Rokeby stood exactly upon the site of the present mansion, by which a part of its walls is enclosed. It is surrounded by a profusion of fine wood, and the park in which it stands is adorned by the junction of the Greta and of

the Tees.' (Scott, *Rokeby: a Poem* [3rd edn, Edinburgh, 1813], pp. 325–6 and 375. I am grateful to Mr J.A. Gamble for drawing my attention to it.) *Rokeby* is a pseudo-historical jumble set in 1644, in the aftermath of the battle of Marston Moor, and Scott was mistaken in thinking that the Rokeby family were still in possession at that time: the estate had actually been sold by a Sir Thomas Rokeby to William Robinson, a London merchant, in 1610 (G.E. C[ockayne], *Complete Peerage ... Extant, Extinct or Dormant* [8 vols, London, 1887–98], VI, p. 391).

In addition to Scott's poem, Rokeby Park is unalterably associated with Velasquez's *Rokeby Venus*. This famous picture, painted *c.*1650, was bought by Scott's friend, J.B.S. Morritt, in 1814, and was the flagship of the 'Morritt Collection'. It was sold to the National Gallery in London in 1906. (Augusto Gentili, William Barcham and Linda Whitley, *Paintings in the National Gallery*, London, 2000, pp. 307, 310–11 and 341. I am grateful for this information to Ms Nova Carlson of the General Reference Section of Belfast Public Library.)

145   Betty Rizzo, *Companions without Vows: Relationships among Eighteenth-Century British Women* (Athens, Georgia, 1994), p. 117. Professor Rizzo's study of Mrs Montagu reveals that she was a hard, cold, adulation-seeking woman, so perhaps this was a Robinson characteristic. Mrs Montagu's estates were supposed to have a rental of £10,000 per annum at her death in 1800 (*Complete Peerage*, VI, 392). She left them to the future 3rd Lord Rokeby. All told, there were six Lords Rokeby. Robinson's cousin, Matthew, the 2nd Lord, was a famous eccentric, who sported a beard of 'patriarchal length' in an era when a beard was 'deemed an unsightly excrescence' (*Public Characters of 1798–9* [4th edn], pp. 554–66; Sir Lewis Namier and John Brooke, *The History of Parliament: the House of Commons, 1754–90* [3 vols, London, 1964], III, pp. 367–8). The 6th and last Lord Rokeby was a Crimean War general. He died without issue in 1883, when the Robinson of Rokeby baronetcy and the barony of Rokeby became extinct.

146   Cowper, *Deans of Canterbury*, pp. 174–7.

147   Craig, *op. cit.*, p. 28.

148   Hillsborough to Buckinghamshire, 20 Jan. 1777, *HMC Lothian Mss.*, p. 298.

149   Stuart, *Armagh*, p. 454.

150   Neely, *op. cit.*

151   Mohan, *op. cit.*, p. 130; Simms, *Primate Robinson*, p. 139.

152   It should, however, be noted that Archbishop Simms is more critical of Robinson in his unpublished lecture to a mainly clerical audience in Armagh in 1971 than he is in his article on Robinson published in *Irish Booklore* in the same year.

153   John Coleman, 'Sir Joshua Reynolds and Richard Robinson, Archbishop of Armagh', in *Irish Arts Review* (1995), pp. 131–6; Mrs Reginald Lane Poole, *Catalogue of Portraits in the Possession of the University, Colleges, City and*

County of Oxford, III (Oxford, 1926), pp. 74–5 (I am indebted for this reference to Dr T.C. Barnard); Nicholas Penny (ed.), *Reynolds* [RA Exhibition Catalogue] (London, 1986), p. 57. In suggesting that the 1763 Reynolds portrait of Robinson may have been intended as a kind of advertisement of Robinson for the primacy, Coleman perhaps forgets that Stone and Robinson were contemporaries. Could Stone's death at the end of 1764 have been foreseen early in 1763?

154   The rest of this paragraph, and most of the next three, are taken from Malcomson, *Archbishop Charles Agar*, pp. 458–61.

155   Simms, *Primate Robinson*, pp. 140–41; Mohan, *op. cit.*, p. 129.

156   General John Pomeroy to his brother, Arthur, later 1st Lord Harberton, 11 Aug. 1782, Pomeroy papers, PRONI, T/2954/4/8.

157   Malcomson, *Archbishop Charles Agar*, pp. 180–82.

158   Pomeroy to Harberton, 25 July 1789, T/2954/4/19; Johnston-Liik, *History of the Irish Parliament*, V, pp. 245–6, and VI, pp. 149–50.

159   For the issue of coadjutorships, see Malcomson, *Archbishop Charles Agar*, pp. 499–504.

INDEX